Teach them to pray:

Cultivating God-dependency in your church

Paul Tautges

©Day One Publications 2010
First printed 2010

Scripture quotations taken from the New American Standard Bible®, Copyright © 1960, 1962, 1963, 1968, 1971, 1972, 1973, 1975, 1977, 1995 by The Lockman Foundation. Used by permission. (www.Lockman.org)

A CIP record is held at the British Library

ISBN 978-1-84625-196-2

Published by Day One Publications, Ryelands Road, Leominster, HR6 8NZ
☎ 01568 613 740
FAX 01568 611 473
email—sales@dayone.co.uk
web site—www.dayone.co.uk
North American e-mail—usasales@dayone.co.uk
North American web site—www.dayonebookstore.com

Cover designed by Wayne McMaster and printed in the USA

To David Ehler, a faithful brother in Christ, whose life-commitment to prayer, as a high priority in the life of the local church, continues to challenge my own heart and to bless the ministry of our church.

ENDORSEMENTS

Paul Tautges has produced yet another small, usable handbook to assist busy pastors in a critical aspect of ministry—the cultivation of a congregational sense of God-dependency expressed through prayer. After underscoring the biblical emphasis on ordinary believers being in constant prayer, Tautges presents seven informative, stimulating prayer-meeting messages, ranging from praying in Jesus's name to praying for unbelievers and government leaders. The heart of the book is then buttressed with several helpful appendixes, providing practical ideas to ministers for stirring up prayer in their local church. The idea of beginning each year with nine days of emphasis on prayer (including four sermons on prayer), in which each family lists reasons for praise and requests for prayer, so that the entire flock learns to pray informatively for one another as a church family, is just one of several exciting possibilities. Use Teach Them to Pray *as a springboard to cultivate your own ideas on how you, as a pastor or church leader, can cultivate prayer in your church in our day of widespread prayerlessness and spiritual amnesia.*

Dr. Joel R. Beeke, President, Puritan Reformed Theological Seminary, Grand Rapids, Michigan, USA

[There] is something sacred about the corporate prayer of believers. This emphasis makes Paul Tautges' book a valuable contribution to our theology and practice of prayer. Paul Tautges not only encourages us to pray corporately, but he also instructs us to pray biblically. [Much] of the corporate prayer we do engage in is basically centered on our own health and financial needs. By contrast, Paul Tautges directs us to the prayers of the Bible, which are basically God-centered. All of us need encouragement and instruction in the discipline of corporate prayer, and this book will help us to that end.

Jerry Bridges, international speaker and best-selling author, The Pursuit of Holiness

A WORD OF THANKS

I thank David Ehler, to whom this book is dedicated, for the steadfast love, encouragement, and dedication to prayer that he has modeled for me, and the rest of my church, the past eighteen years of my ministry as the pastor of Immanuel Bible Church in Sheboygan, Wisconsin. "Older men are to be temperate, dignified, sensible, sound in faith, in love, in perseverance" (Titus 2:2).

I thank my faithful wife, Karen, for her continued encouragement to keep writing and for never complaining about being the wife of a busy pastor. No more patient or suitable helper for this difficult man, and more capable mother to our ten wonderful children, could be found on this earth. "Her children rise up and bless her; her husband also" (Prov. 31:28–29).

I thank my oldest daughter, Ashley, for her assistance in transcribing the sermons that formed the initial content of the book, and for the consistent honor she expresses toward me. "I have no greater joy than this, to hear of my children walking in the truth" (3 John 1:4).

I again thank my brother-in-law and sister, Kurt and Jean Kielisch, for the use of their cottage on Green Lake as a writing retreat. "Love is kind" (1 Cor. 13:4).

I again thank Jim Holmes of Day One Publications for his enthusiasm for the Ministering the Master's Way series; and Suzanne Mitchell for her assistance as my gracious editor. Both of these servants have encouraged me immensely. "As each one has received a special gift, employ it in serving one another as good stewards of the manifold grace of God" (1 Peter 4:10).

Last, but not least, I thank Dr. Joel Beeke for his kind review and endorsement; and I thank Jerry Bridges, my unseen mentor since my infant days as a believer, for his kindness in writing the Foreword to this book. I am truly honored by this demonstration of grace. "Therefore encourage one another and build up one another, just as you also are doing" (1 Thes. 5:11).

CONTENTS

FOREWORD

Why another book on prayer? It seems a new book on prayer appears so often to take its place alongside other books that have been on our shelves for a long time. So why another one? I can think of three reasons.

First, we need to be continually reminded of the basic truths of Scripture, especially in this day when we all experience information-overload. We forget so easily unless we are constantly reminded. It was for this reason that, even in the early days of the New Testament church, the Apostle Peter wrote in 2 Peter 1:12, "Therefore, I will always be ready to remind you of these things, even though you already know them, and have been established in the truth which is present with you." And this reminder is especially needed in the area of prayer.

Second, prayer is hard work. Paul calls it "striving" (Rom. 15:30) and "laboring earnestly" (Col. 4:12). Even Bible study and, for the pastor or teacher, message preparation seem easier to do than to struggle in prayer. So we need continual encouragement to pray.

Third, and this reason is unique to this book, *Teach Them to Pray: Cultivating God-Dependency in Your Church* is directed primarily toward corporate prayer in the context of the local church. My observation is that most books on prayer tend to focus on our individual prayer lives, and even in that area we need to be reminded, instructed, and exhorted. But the whole idea of corporate prayer seems to be gradually disappearing, even among our Bible-centered evangelical churches.

We proliferate our programs while at the same time we marginalize corporate prayer. The old-fashioned Wednesday night prayer meeting has virtually disappeared. And though there is nothing sacred about Wednesday night as a prayer-meeting time, there certainly is something sacred about the corporate prayer of believers. This emphasis makes Paul Tautges' book a valuable contribution to our theology and practice of prayer.

Paul Tautges not only encourages us to pray corporately, but he also instructs us to pray biblically. Again, my observation is that much of the corporate prayer we do engage in is basically centered on our own health and financial needs. By contrast, Pastor Tautges directs us to the prayers of the Bible, which are basically God-centered.

Though this book is directed primarily at pastors, it will prove valuable to all members of a congregation. All of us need encouragement and instruction in the discipline of corporate prayer, and this book will help us to that end.

Jerry Bridges,
International speaker and best-selling
author, *The Pursuit of Holiness*

INTRODUCTION

A life of prayer is irrefutable proof of God-dependency. This is true not only of the individual believer, but also of the local church, as evidenced in the New Testament historical accounts and the epistles. Churches therefore need to learn how to pray. But who will teach them? As pastors and elders we must not only tell the members of our flocks to pray, we must also teach them how to bring their needs to God's throne of grace. We must regularly instruct them in the biblical principles, examples, and commands concerning a life of prayer. In short, our churches need a biblical theology of prayer—a God-centered way of thinking as it relates to speaking to our Creator and our Redeemer. This will only develop when we commit ourselves to the faithful teaching of all that God has revealed in His Word concerning prayer.

Prayer is the only form of communication with God available to the believer. It is crucial, therefore, that we understand how God wills for us to speak with Him. R. L. Dabney (1820–1898) defined prayer as "an offering up of our desires unto God for things agreeable to His will, in the name of Christ, with confession of our sins, and thankful acknowledgement of His mercies."[1] Since our hearts are utterly depraved and able to corrupt even our most sincere intentions (Jer. 17:9), the only means by which we may hope to ask God "for things agreeable to His will" is by learning to pray according to the revelation of His will contained in His written Word. Anything else presumes on God. Dabney concurs:

> The proper rule of prayer is the whole Word of God. Not only are its instances of inspired devotion our exemplars, and its promises our warrant; its precepts are the measure of our petitions, and its threatenings the stimulants. There is no part of Scripture which may

not minister to the guidance of the Christian's prayers. But further, the Word of God is the rule of our prayers also in this sense, that all which it does not authorize, is excluded. Prayer being a homage to God, it is for Him to say what worship He will accept; all else is not homage, but presumption.[2]

Scripture has more to say about prayer than we can ever hope to master in one lifetime. Hence, a desire to continually be taught how to pray is a mark of growth toward spiritual maturity. The more a believer grows in Christ, the less he or she is governed by a spirit of independence and the more his or her life becomes marked by habitual God-dependency.

This book is submitted as an aid to fellow ministers of the gospel, to challenge us to go beyond telling believers to pray more, to teaching them how to think biblically about prayer and about the God to whom we pray. All in all, it is the author's hope that local churches will be strengthened and energized by a renewed commitment to the constancy of prayer.

Part 1
Prayer—an expression of God-dependency

In the first two chapters I begin to demonstrate that prayer was the very lifeblood of the New Testament church; that is, the early believers in Christ truly lived out an attitude of God-dependency. Prayer, not self-sufficiency, was their habitual practice. That is, they did not trust in their own abilities, or in their cleverness and wisdom, but on the power of God to accomplish His mighty work through the Spirit and the gospel. However, this confidence in the instrumental causes of salvation (the Word and the Spirit) did not leave them passive, waiting for God to act; rather they became active in the labor of communication with Him by means of fervent prayer. Their example, as preserved for us in the Scriptures, testifies that they wholeheartedly believed the words of Jesus when He said, "apart from Me you can do nothing" (John 15:5), prayer being one of the chief evidences of their constant abiding in Christ.

Chapter 1 takes a peek into a Jerusalem prayer meeting as the believers gather in one heart and one mind to seek the Lord. This look at a historical narrative in the Book of Acts reveals the role of prayer in transforming common believers into uncommon servants whose humble yet passionate and unified dependence upon God contributes to the display of His glory.

Chapter 2 examines three quick-fire commands from the Apostle Paul, which are interconnected expressions of God-dependency, at the end of his first epistle to the believers in Thessalonica. It is almost as if the apostle, as he puts the finishing touches to his letter, quickly reminds his readers of some bare essentials of communion with God. Today, our churches desperately need to heed this apostolic instruction.

Common people in constant prayer (Acts 1:12–14)

The outstanding thing about these men is that they were not outstanding.

–Kenneth O. Gangel

How sad is the state of the modern church relative to the practice of whole-church prayer! Robert Duncan Culver laments,

> This is a day of going and doing, of activity. The mid-week prayer meeting has largely been lost in the contest for a slot in the weekly schedule when people are free to attend. Everything else seems more important. The old time mid-weekly prayer routines are not sacred, nor are the time-worn methods of proclaiming the Word, but proclamation and prayer are at the heart of the Savior's program for His church. They dare not be laid aside. If we have scheduled them out we must again schedule them in. The forms may change, but the essentials must not be neglected and lost.[1]

Though prayerlessness may be very apparent in Christianity today, prayer was not an afterthought to the New Testament church. Far from being a leftover offered to God once their primary energies had been dispensed on the "more urgent" activities of church life, prayer was considered by the early believers to be a staple they could not live without. They were truly God-dependent people.

This is obvious from the foundation-forming days of the church. Immediately following Jesus's ascension to the right hand of God, the disciples obeyed His last command to wait for the Holy Spirit at least in part by devoting themselves to prayer, as witnessed by Acts 1:12–14. As we examine this passage of Scripture, it is as if we climb a stepladder in order to peek into the second-story window of a house in Jerusalem. There we see a large room where the disciples have gathered for one purpose—to pray.

> Then they returned to Jerusalem from the mount called Olivet, which is near Jerusalem, a Sabbath day's journey away. When they had entered the city, they went up to the upper room where they were staying; that is, Peter and John and James and Andrew, Philip and Thomas, Bartholomew and Matthew, James the son of Alphaeus, and Simon the Zealot, and Judas the son of James. These all with one mind were continually devoting themselves to prayer, along with the women, and Mary the mother of Jesus, and with His brothers.

> Acts 1:12–14

Our observation of this Jerusalem prayer meeting focuses on three elements: a common place, filled with common people, who are involved in constant prayer.

Common place (v. 12)

First, we see the believers gathered in a common place. Verse 12 reads, "Then they returned to Jerusalem from the mount called Olivet, which is near Jerusalem, a Sabbath day's journey away. When they had entered the city, they went up to the upper room where they were staying." Gathered in this second-story room are the eyewitnesses of the ascension, which took place on "the mount called Olivet." They have returned to Jerusalem just as Jesus commanded them (Acts 1:4), having descended 200 feet from the mount to Jerusalem, a journey providing a magnificent view of the city. According to Luke, they were on the mountain near Bethany (Luke 24:50), a "Sabbath day's journey away." This does not mean the event occurred on a Sabbath, since Jesus ascended on a Thursday forty days after His resurrection. The phrase "a Sabbath day's journey" was a measurement of time, or better, of distance. It referred to the distance the Jewish rabbis considered acceptable for travel on a Sabbath: 2,000 cubits or about three-fourths of a mile. Jewish historian Josephus confirms the distance of the Mount of Olives as being 3,000 feet, or 2,000 cubits, from Jerusalem.[2] This limited distance was first established in the Old Testament, when all Israel was encamped around the tabernacle. No tent was placed further than 2,000 cubits away.

The upper room where the believers gathered was a large space in a house where they were "staying," and apparently a regular meeting place for the purpose of prayer. The use of the definite article "the" ("the upper room") seems to indicate that it was probably the same upper room where they had shared the Last Supper with Jesus (Mark 14:12–26) and where the Lord gave his promise to send the Holy Spirit, for whom they were now waiting (Acts 1:8). It was in this place that the disciples joined their hearts and minds together for the purpose of prayer.

Common people (vv. 13–14)

Second, from the top of our ladder we observe common people: "Peter and John and James and Andrew, Philip and Thomas, Bartholomew and Matthew, James the son of Alphaeus, and Simon the Zealot, and Judas the son of James … along with the women, and Mary the mother of Jesus, and with His brothers" (1:13–14). Along with these there were enough brethren to form a prayer meeting 120 people strong. In particular, the Eleven were there, listed in the same way as in Luke 6:14–16 but in a different order and without Judas, for by this time he had hung himself (Acts 1:16–18).

Peter, John, and James are probably listed first because Luke had already planned to focus on their ministries later in his book. Peter and John were fishermen. Peter is always listed first in the biblical record, no doubt in recognition of his budding leadership. John, the younger brother of James, was one of the "sons of thunder" known for their religious zeal. He is often called "the apostle of love" or the one "whom Jesus loved," due to the close relationship he had with Jesus (John 13:23), which shines through in his writings. John wrote much about love in his three epistles (1, 2, and 3 John), and much about Christ in the Book of Revelation. James, the brother of John, was also a common fisherman who later became the chief leader in the church of Jerusalem and was ultimately killed by Herod (Acts 12:2).

Andrew was another fisherman, being the brother of Simon Peter. It was Andrew who was called by Jesus first and who then found Peter and said, "We have found the Messiah," bringing Peter to Jesus (John 1:41–42). Andrew was the quiet one who lived in the shadow of his big brother.

Philip was probably also a common fisherman. In John 6:7 we find him exasperated at the sight of 5,000 hungry men and their families: "Two hundred denarii worth of bread is not enough to feed this crowd." Though sometimes lacking in faith, Philip later became a successful evangelist (Acts 8).

Thomas, also known as "The Twin," will forever go down in history as "Doubting Thomas." Absent from the upper room when the resurrected Jesus made His first appearance to the Eleven (John 20:24), Thomas refused to believe their testimony that Jesus had risen from the grave. Eight days later, Jesus, abounding in patience, said to Thomas, "Reach here with your finger, and see My hands; and reach here your hand and put it into My side; and do not be unbelieving, but believing" (John 20:27).

Bartholomew is another name for Nathanael. He was born in Cana, where Jesus performed His first miracle of turning water into wine (John 2:1–11). Bartholomew was a friend of Philip, who brought him to Jesus (John 1:45).

Matthew was a tax collector (Matt. 10:3). As such, he lived in the lower class of society along with other undesirables, fellow tax collectors, and common sinners.

James, the son of Alphaeus, is also referred to as "James the Less" (Mark 15:40). All we really know about him is his name. He was not a prominent guy.

Simon was a member of a political party known as the Zealots (Matt. 10:4). The desire of this Jewish group was to take over society. They had hoped that the Messiah would come to help them overthrow the Romans and aid them in their fierce advocacy of Mosaic ritual.

Judas the son of James was also known as Thaddaeus (Mark 3:18). Judas appears in the Gospels as a tender-hearted, humble kind of man.

So what is the point of all this? The point is that these now-famous men were nothing more than mere men, yet they were God-dependent men, men whom the Spirit of God used mightily to advance the cause of the gospel. Of these eleven disciples, Kenneth Gangel writes, "The outstanding thing about these men is that they were not outstanding. God chose ordinary men to do an extraordinary task."[3] Chosen not for their innate qualities or natural abilities, these common men remain examples of God's choice of those whom the world views as least likely to succeed. This, the Apostle Paul argues, is for the purpose of making God's power and glory more obvious:

> For consider your calling, brethren, that there were not many wise according to the flesh, not many mighty, not many noble; but God has chosen the foolish things of the world to shame the wise, and God has chosen the weak things of the world to shame the things which are strong, and the base things of the world and the despised God has chosen, the things that are not, so that He may nullify the things that are, so that no man may boast before God.
>
> 1 Cor. 1:26–29

One of the pleasures of God is to take ordinary, common

sinners, redeem them, and then empower them with the Spirit to walk in God-dependency. And the clearest mark of their humble, God-dependent spirit is their dedication to prayer.

Praying with these eleven ordinary men were also "the women," undoubtedly the ones who followed Jesus from Galilee. Included were Mary Magdalene, Mary the wife of Clopas, Mary and Martha, Salome, and others. Mary "the mother of Jesus" is also mentioned here for the last time in the Scriptures.

The brothers of Jesus, who until recently had been unbelievers, were also present at this Jerusalem prayer meeting. Approximately six months prior to the crucifixion of Jesus, it was said of them that "not even His brothers were believing in Him" (John 7:5). They are listed in Mark 6:3 as James, Joses, Judas, and Simon. Two—James and Judas (Jude)—wrote portions of Scripture, both referring to themselves as "bond-servants" of Jesus Christ (James 1:1; Jude 1:1). The absence of a reference to their family relationship to Jesus in the introductions to their letters provides an insight into their meekness and servanthood. These men had no desire to be big shots, but rather yearned only to love and serve the One they had denied for so long. It was common people like these toward whom God turned His listening ear as they devoted themselves to prayer.

Constant prayer (v. 14)

Third—and most applicable to the conviction of this book— while peering through the window, we observe their loyalty to prayer. All 120 of them were "with one mind ... continually devoting themselves to prayer." During the ten days between the ascension of Jesus and the feast of Pentecost the believers attended to prayer. This does not mean that they prayed nonstop; Luke 24:52–53 indicates that they were also praising God in the temple and freely moving about the city. But we may suppose, as some commentators do, that they gathered at their common meeting place at least once a day for prayer. What they specifically prayed for is not mentioned, although the context suggests a few matters that must have been on their minds: the wait for the promise of the Spirit, the command to become worldwide witnesses for Christ, the need to replace Judas, and the preparations for the feast of Pentecost. Most noteworthy is the habit that prayer had already become for the early believers. This is made clear by two characteristics.

PASSIONATELY UNIFIED IN MIND

First, the unity of the believers in prayer is clearly evident. Verse 14 indicates that they all prayed "with one mind," which means "with one accord," or "with one passion." They were in complete agreement as to the commission Jesus had placed upon them, and were determined to obey His instructions to remain in Jerusalem until the coming of the Holy Spirit. This tight unity among the early Christians is apparent throughout the Book of Acts.

We read, for example, that they continued day by day "with one mind" in fellowship and communion (2:46), and that they prayed for boldness "with one accord" (4:24). Also, many signs and wonders took place while they were all together "with one accord" (5:12). The apostles and elders were also "of one mind" at the Jerusalem Council concerning the doctrinal correction that was needed and consequently selected and sent forth messengers to deliver their decision to the brethren at Antioch (15:25).

This same unity should mark believers in Christ today. Ephesians 4:3 exhorts us to be "diligent to preserve the unity of the Spirit in the bond of peace" as part of walking in a manner worthy of the calling of God in the gospel. Notice that we are not called to *create* a unity that does not exist, such as a superficial unity without doctrinal agreement, but to *preserve* the unity that the Spirit has already knit among true believers in Christ.

As we submit to the Spirit of God by submitting to His Word, we are united in mind for the labor of prayer. And as likeminded believers pray together, God knits their hearts together in deeper affection and empowers them to accomplish His work. For this reason, Paul writes this benediction toward the end of his letter to the Romans: "Now may the God who gives perseverance and encouragement grant you to be of the same mind with one another according to Christ Jesus" (Rom. 15:5). Paul was convinced that the same God who produces endurance in the hearts of believers would also join their truth-informed minds together in order that they might "with one voice glorify the God and Father of our Lord Jesus Christ" (Rom. 15:6).

EARNESTLY DEVOTED TO PRAYER

Second, the devotion to corporate prayer of those early believers is obvious and intense: "These all with one mind were *continually devoting* themselves to prayer." This habit of constantly attending to prayer flowed from an earnest commitment to biblical priorities, which again is a pattern in the early church. For example, according to Acts 2:42, the believers were "continually devoting themselves to the apostles' teaching and to fellowship, to the breaking of bread and to prayer." The essential aspects of their life as a church family included being continually devoted to doctrine (teaching), to fellowship (community), the Lord's Table (cross-centeredness), and to prayer (God-dependency). Later, the apostles confirmed the priority of prayer by the example they set when they assigned the solving of ministry conflicts to other godly men (Acts 6:1–7). The apostles' reasoning is clearly stated: "But *we will devote ourselves* to prayer and to the ministry of the word" (v. 4, emphasis added).

In our day, it is common for local churches that experience numerical growth to become so filled with people-related activities that prayer gradually gets marginalized, but this did not occur among the early believers. As the church continued to expand, their commitment to whole-church prayer did not waver. For example, three areas of ministry were immediately impacted by their devotion to prayer. First, major turns in missionary outreach flowed out of their constant attention to prayer. It was when "Peter went up on the housetop about the sixth hour to pray" that God called him to take the gospel to the house of Cornelius (Acts 10:9), thus opening a major gate to the evangelism of the Gentile world. Second, supernatural deliverance from persecution came as a direct result of a church-wide prayer meeting: "So Peter was kept in the prison, but prayer for him was being made fervently by the church to God" (12:5; 6–17). When he was supernaturally delivered, Peter knew exactly where to turn to first: to the house "where many were gathered together and were praying" (v. 12). Third, the matter of selecting and affirming the first missionaries came about "While they were ministering to the Lord and fasting" (13:1–3), undoubtedly with prayer since the disciplines of prayer and fasting usually accompany each other (see Ps. 35:13; Dan. 9:3; Matt. 6:6–18; 17:21).

To the early church, regular prayer meetings were an indispensable part of their very existence. As J. C. Ryle writes, "Prayer is to faith what breath is to life. How a man can live and not breathe is past my comprehension, and how a man can believe and not pray is past my comprehension too."[4] The early believers simply could not fathom a Christian community existing without the habit of prayer. As a result, God often supernaturally intervened on their behalf.

This brief survey of the early church's life of prayer demonstrates that we cannot survive without prayer. Devotion to prayer turns common people into uncommon servants of God. For that reason, we need to be constantly devoted to prayer. God is delighted when His people join their truth-informed minds and hearts together in the common bond of prayer.

➡ Teach them to pray

This book has grown out of the conviction that if our congregations do not learn to pray biblically, we will not effectively carry out the will of God. We must therefore teach them to pray. We must train common believers to be God-dependent people who constantly cry out to God for His will to be done on earth as it is done in heaven.

Constant prayer and the will of God (1 Thes. 5:16–18)

Because prayer is an attitude of dependency, the one who really prays is *submissive*, submissive to the Divine will.

–A. W. Pink

The pointed command to "pray without ceasing" (1 Thes. 5:17) should startle us. For who among us prays continually? The very idea sounds preposterous. "Without ceasing" sounds like tireless activity requiring endurance and lifetime commitment. It sounds like a habit that is not only good and helpful, but also essential to our very existence. Such is the case with prayer and the believer. This same conviction led Martin Luther to state, "To be a Christian without prayer is no more possible than to be alive without breathing."[1] Just as the expansion and contraction of our lungs is necessary for the continuance of our physical life, so regular fellowship with God in prayer is essential to our spiritual well-being. Without prayer our spiritual lives will shrivel up and return to an infantile state.

The verses that surround this brief command to "pray without ceasing" reveal it is less abrupt than it seems at first: "Rejoice always; pray without ceasing; in everything give thanks; for this is God's will for you in Christ Jesus" (1 Thes. 5:16–18). These verses actually contain three separate, but related, commands which stress the importance of maintaining a habitual lifestyle of God-dependency. As an expression of our reliance upon God, prayer is an essential aspect of fulfilling God's will for our lives.

Rejoice always (v. 16)

The first command in the passage is clear: "Rejoice always." "Rejoice" comes from *chairo*, meaning "to be glad" or "to delight in." The only other occurrence of this word is found in Philippians 4:4 where it is used twice: "Rejoice in the Lord always; again I will say, rejoice!" In each case it appears in the form of a command, which means this inner state of gladness is a choice. In light of this, it is vital that we understand what it means to rejoice in the Lord always.

REJOICE ALWAYS—EVEN IN TRIALS (JAMES 1:2–3)

The idea of rejoicing at all times runs against the grain of our humanity. Our depravity has trained us to believe that joy is the same as happiness and is dependent upon our circumstances. If life is going well by our standards, we are joyful, but if circumstances take a turn for the worse, we believe we have a right to allow our joy to dissolve in the muddy waters of our suffering. However, that is not so, for the command is "Rejoice *always*."

James affirms this same truth when he writes, "Consider it all joy, my brethren, when you encounter various trials, knowing that the testing of your faith produces endurance" (James 1:2–3). James does not teach us to wait until our particular manner of suffering is over in order to rejoice, but rather to rejoice *when* we encounter various trials—*during* our suffering. The word "consider" is a command which calls for a certain outlook; that is, it is our duty to pursue an attitude of joy in the midst of trials. This joy is not an emotion that arises from the trial itself, but is a secure peace that comes from knowing that God's good and perfect will is sure to be carried out as a result of the hardship. God desires our faith to be accompanied by the character quality of endurance. Therefore, He appoints suffering to breed this trait.

James is not telling us, "No matter how painful your suffering is, just put on a happy face. Pretend, if you have to. Whatever you do, don't let anyone know you are really hurting." He is not suggesting we live in denial. Trials are hard. Trials do hurt. The inner pain is at times seemingly unbearable. But the joy of the Lord is our strength (Neh. 8:10). Therefore, we can—and must—rejoice always. This is God's will for every believer.

REJOICE ALWAYS—IN THE LORD (PHIL. 4:4)

Again, it is not our circumstances that form the basis of Christian joy. The apostle was in prison when he exhorted the Philippians to "Rejoice in the Lord always; again I will say, rejoice!" (Phil. 4:4). True joy is found *in the Lord*. For joy to be present in our hearts the Lord must be our focal point. As long as the eyes of our faith are fixed upon our troubles we will not find joy. Until our minds consciously move the Lord from our peripheral vision into the narrow corridor of our focus, joy will elude us.

This kind of God-centered focus is illustrated best by the psalmist's resolve, "I have set the Lord continually before me; because He is at my right hand, I will not be shaken" (Ps. 16:8). Psalm 16 begins and ends with prayer (see vv. 1–2, 10–11). This man did not set his *troubles* before his mind's eye. Nor did he dwell on his fears or the many "what if"s of life. Instead, he made the conscious choice to place the Lord, His faithfulness as Protector, and His sufficiency for his life before his face "continually." This determined focus was a chosen habit which took root within the soil of communion with God in prayer. The psalmist's attitude of God-dependency fueled his joy: "Therefore my heart is glad and my glory rejoices; my flesh also will dwell securely" (Ps. 16:9). The connection between prayer and rejoicing is inescapable. As a result, the psalmist's faith could not be shaken, nor could his joy be stolen away from him.

Pray constantly (v. 17)

The second command found in 1 Thessalonians 5:16–18 is "pray without ceasing." The Greek word translated "without ceasing" is *adialeiptos*, which means "without interruption," "unceasingly," or "constantly." The *Linguistic Key to the Greek New Testament* indicates, "The word was used of that which was continually and repeatedly done; e.g. the uninterrupted necessary payment of hard taxes; the continual service or

31

ministry of an official; a continual uninterrupted cough."[2] All three images imply continual—even nagging—action.

Since "pray without ceasing" is a command from the apostle we are certain it remains the will of God that we remain committed to prayer as an essential discipline of the Christian life, as the very next verse explicitly says: "*this is God's will* for you in Christ Jesus" (v. 18, emphasis added). Prayer is the only means whereby we may speak to God. God communicates with us through His Word, but we communicate with Him by means of prayer. Clearly, then, it is God's will for us to express our dependence upon Him through constant communication with Him in prayer.

The prophet Samuel recognized prayer as part of the will of God. When the people of Israel realized the sinfulness of their demand for a human king in the place of God's sovereign rule, they begged Samuel to intercede for them: "Pray for your servants to the Lord your God, so that we may not die, for we have added to all our sins this evil by asking for ourselves a king" (1 Sam. 12:19). In response, Samuel exhorted them to return to God lest they again turn away to futile things. However, he also understood his own personal responsibility to continue to pray for them: "Moreover, as for me, far be it from me that I should sin against the Lord by ceasing to pray for you; but I will instruct you in the good and right way" (v. 23). The Hebrew word translated "ceasing" is *hadal*, which carries the meaning of stopping, neglecting, or refraining from doing something. Though the people of Israel behaved rebelliously, their faithful prophet refused to neglect prayer on their behalf. He refused to give up on them. Israel had clearly stepped out of the will of God, but Samuel was determined that he would not do the same. Instead, he recommitted himself to pray for his people as part of his own obedience to God.

It is critical for us to recognize this truth: Samuel called prayerlessness *sin*. How many of us are willing to do the same?

Oh, we feel badly when our prayer lives become stagnant or virtually nonexistent. But do we call our lack of prayer *sin* and repent of it as a form of independence from God? We are ready to admit, sometimes even with a degree of spiritual pride, that we need others to pray for us because "we are struggling in our prayer lives." But which of us dares to stand in church and publicly declare, "I must confess to you my sin of prayerlessness. I need you to pray for me to truly repent of this sin. Please hold me accountable to my renewed commitment to a lifestyle of God-dependent prayer"? Prayerlessness is sin, as is the self-sufficient heart attitude of independence that feeds it. In his classic work *The Sovereignty of God*, A. W. Pink writes,

> Prayer is not so much an act as it is an *attitude*—an attitude of *dependency*, dependency upon God. Prayer is confession of creature weakness, yea, of helplessness ... Therefore, prayer is the very opposite of *dictating* to God. Because prayer is an attitude of dependency, the one who really prays is *submissive*, submissive to the Divine will; and submission to the Divine will means that we are content for the Lord to supply our need according to the dictates of His own sovereign pleasure.[3]

Prayerlessness is the most subtle disclosure of our independence from God and is our depraved heart's own declaration of sovereignty. Beware of the subtle sin of prayerlessness! We must commit ourselves anew to a lifestyle of constant prayer, which will keep us in a state of submission to the will of God. There are two aspects of the divine will that we must ponder, as they relate to the need to practice constant prayer.

Constant prayer protects us from temptation (Mark 14:38)

In Mark 14:38, Jesus exhorts His disciples, "Keep watching and praying that you may not come into temptation; the spirit is willing, but the flesh is weak." The previous verse reads, "And He came and found them sleeping, and said to Peter, 'Simon, are you asleep? Could you not keep watch for one hour?'" While Jesus was preparing to die, His disciples were sleeping! If we are honest we will quickly admit how much we are like they were.

The principle taught by Jesus is clear: Lack of diligence in prayer leaves us in a vulnerable position, making us easy prey for temptation. He called the disciples, and thereby us, to constant prayer, "*that* [we] may not come into temptation." Prayer is necessary to keep us spiritually alert to the weakness of our own flesh and its propensity to sin. Lehman Straus writes, "No one can both sin and pray. True prayer will prevent us from sinning, or sin will prevent us from praying."[4] Jesus had taught His followers to pray, "And do not lead us into temptation" (Matt. 6:13). A lifestyle of dependence upon God in prayer guards our hearts from temptation and keeps us spiritually alert rather than lying in slumber, vulnerable to sin's allure.

CONSTANT PRAYER KEEPS US ALERT TO THE ATTACKS OF THE DEVIL (EPH. 6:18)

In addition to his first letter to the Thessalonian church, there is another place in the New Testament where the Apostle Paul calls his readers to constant prayer. To the church at Ephesus he writes, "With all prayer and petition *pray at all times* in the Spirit, and with this in view, be on the alert with all perseverance and petition for all the saints" (Eph. 6:18, emphasis added). We are to pray constantly "with this in view." With what in view? With an awareness of the reality of spiritual warfare, which he has just described in the previous eight verses (6:10–17).

Peter also makes the same connection between prayer and spiritual alertness in the Christian's war when he exhorts, "The end of all things is near; therefore, be of sound judgment and sober spirit for the purpose of prayer" (1 Peter 4:7). Included in the "all things" that Peter has in mind are the diabolical ways of the devil, whose agenda is to destroy Christians, for Peter again calls us to spiritual alertness in the very next chapter: "Be of sober spirit, be on the alert. Your adversary, the devil, prowls around like a roaring lion, seeking someone to devour. But resist him, firm in your faith, knowing that the same experiences of suffering are being accomplished by your brethren who are in the world" (5:8–9). Surely a significant part of our resistance to the attacks and temptations of the devil is a healthy dependence upon God's strength expressed most obviously through prayer. John Piper writes of the importance of prayer in the spiritual war:

> Prayer is the walkie-talkie on the battlefield of the world. It calls on God for courage (Ephesians 6:19). It calls in for troop deployment and target location (Acts 13:1–3). It calls in for protection and air cover (Matthew 6:13; Luke 21:36). It calls in for firepower to blast open a way for the Word (Colossians 4:3). It calls in for the miracle of healing for the wounded soldiers (James 5:16). It calls in for supplies for the forces (Matthew 6:11; Philippians 4:6). And it calls in for needed reinforcements (Matthew 9:38). This is the place of prayer—on the battlefield of the world. It is a wartime walkie-talkie for spiritual warfare, not a domestic intercom to increase the comfort of the saints. And one of the reasons it malfunctions in the hands of so many Christian soldiers is that they have gone awol … God has given us prayer because Jesus has given us a mission. God's pleasure in the prayers of his people is proportionate to his passion for world evangelization. We are on this earth to press back the forces of darkness, and we are given access to Headquarters by prayer in order to advance this cause. When we try to turn it into a civilian intercom to increase our material comforts, it malfunctions, and our faith begins to falter.[5]

How do we view prayer? Is it a "domestic intercom" wired to God for the purpose of increasing our personal comforts? Or do we see it as our "wartime walkie-talkie" because we are convinced the Lord of the church has called us to be soldiers on the battlefield of this world? Our understanding of the reality of spiritual warfare greatly influences whether or not we will develop the habit of God-dependent prayer. Remaining in the will of God by remaining in prayer protects us from fleshly temptations as well as Satan's insidious opposition.

Give thanks in all things (v. 18)

The third command is "in everything give thanks." We must be told this because by nature we are not thankful people. It is more natural for sinners like us to complain and to be ungrateful. Regrettably, Jerry Bridges is correct when he writes, "We are anxious to receive but too careless to give thanks. We pray for God's intervention in our lives, then congratulate ourselves rather than God for the results."[6] Therefore, we must discipline ourselves to practice the discipline of thanksgiving. Maintaining an attitude of thanksgiving expressed through constant prayer provides at least six benefits.

THANKFUL PRAYER REMINDS US THAT GOD IS OUR PROVIDER (1 TIM. 4:4–5)

Scripture teaches that all food is from God and therefore should be recognized as such by offering a prayer of thanksgiving to Him: "For everything created by God is good, and nothing is to be rejected if it is received with gratitude; for it is sanctified by means of the word of God and prayer" (1 Tim. 4:4–5). Jesus even modeled this for us in the account of the miraculous feeding of 5,000 men and their families. The Gospel of John is careful to note that before Jesus distributed the loaves and fishes He had already "given thanks" (John 6:11).

As Israel prepared to enter the Promised Land, their faithful shepherd Moses reminded them to be thankful: "When you have eaten and are satisfied, you shall bless the Lord your God for the good land which He has given you" (Deut. 8:10). It is assumed that, because food is God's provision to us, we will bless, or thank, Him for it. When traveling in the former Soviet Union

I always appreciate the believers' dedication to prayer, which is marked by the simple custom of standing to give thanks to God not only *before* a meal, but also *afterward*, prior to anyone leaving the table. This form of thankful prayer is a simple yet important reminder that God is faithful to provide for His children.

THANKFUL PRAYER BRINGS GLORY TO GOD (2 COR. 9:12–15)

One of the reasons why Paul wrote his second letter to the Corinthian church was to challenge them to get back on track concerning their giving to the Lord's work. False apostles, who attacked Paul's leadership by accusing him of being in the ministry for the money, had led the believers astray. Therefore, Paul called them to follow the example of the Macedonian believers, whose sacrificial giving had become well known. He believed with all his heart that "he who sows sparingly will also reap sparingly, and he who sows bountifully will also reap bountifully" (2 Cor. 9:6). The apostle identified one aspect of this bountiful harvest as the thankfulness that the believers' giving produced in the hearts of the recipients and, ultimately, the glory that was received by God:

> For the ministry of this service is not only fully supplying the needs of the saints, but is also overflowing through many thanksgivings to God. Because of the proof given by this ministry, they will glorify God for your obedience to your confession of the gospel of Christ and for the liberality of your contribution to them and to all, while they also, by prayer on your behalf, yearn for you because of the surpassing grace of God in you. Thanks be to God for His indescribable gift!
>
> 2 Cor. 9:12–15

Because these believers were sensitive and generous toward meeting the needs within the Lord's work, their giving overflowed "through many thanksgivings to God." Their love for the brethren, expressed through their giving, caused the recipients to glorify God for His abundant grace. When God meets our needs, thanksgiving should well up in our hearts, producing expressions of gratitude declared to God in prayer, which brings Him both pleasure and glory.

Thankful prayer proves we are filled with the Spirit (Eph. 5:18–20)

Believers are not to be controlled by alcohol (or, by application of principle, any other foreign substance): "do not get drunk with wine," but instead "be filled with the Spirit" (Eph 5:18). To be filled with the Holy Spirit means to be willingly controlled by Him by means of daily submission to the Word of God which He inspired. When this is true we speak "to one another in psalms and hymns and spiritual songs, singing and making melody with [our] heart to the Lord" (v. 19), and we also give "thanks for all things in the name of our Lord Jesus Christ to God, even the Father" (v. 20).

Thankful prayer combats anxiety and invites peace (Phil. 4:6–7)

Thankfulness is a mindset; it is a choice. As such, it is a remedy for worry. Philippians 4:6–7 instructs us to "Be anxious for nothing, but in everything by prayer and supplication with thanksgiving let your requests be made known to God. And the peace of God, which surpasses all comprehension, will guard your hearts and your minds in Christ Jesus." Why did Paul add the words "with thanksgiving"? It is because an anxious spirit cannot coexist with a thankful one. Thankful prayer summons the security guard called *peace* to stand post at the doors of our hearts, forcing out worry and forbidding its reentrance. Thankfulness is the proper attitude of prayer: "Devote yourselves to prayer, keeping alert in it with an *attitude of thanksgiving*" (Col. 4:2, emphasis added).

Thankful prayer reminds us that Christ alone qualifies us to be God's children (Col. 1:12)

The Apostle Paul frequently prayed for the spiritual growth of believers under his care. At the end of his list of the spiritual qualities that he asked God to produce in the hearts of the Colossians is that they would always give "thanks to the Father, who has qualified [them] to share in the inheritance of the saints in Light" (Col. 1:12). When we pray we must never forget that the only reason why God hears us is because Jesus, our Mediator and Advocate, intercedes for us at that very moment (1 Tim. 2:5; 1 John 2:1; Heb. 7:25). Though we are sinners by nature, thought, and deed, God graciously receives us through faith in the sacrificial death and bodily resurrection of His dearly beloved Son. Thankfulness protects us from the prideful thought that we possess even an ounce of virtue in and of ourselves that obligates God to listen to us. We come to God's throne of grace in prayer because of Christ and Christ alone (Heb. 4:15).

THANKFUL PRAYER RECOGNIZES GOD AS THE SOURCE OF STRENGTH (1 TIM. 1:12)

In times of weakness we discover just how strong the strength of God is. This is a lesson God taught Paul by permitting Satan to afflict him with a "thorn in the flesh," which the apostle repeatedly pleaded with God to remove. However, although Satan's goal is always to kill and to destroy, God had certain plans to use that thorn to further the development of Christlike character in the apostle. God knew that Paul was susceptible to the pride of self-sufficiency and therefore he needed to learn that the strength of God was made perfect in His servant's "weakness" (2 Cor. 12:9).

In addition to his own personal struggles, Paul faced severe treatment from others: "we are afflicted in every way, but not crushed; perplexed, but not despairing; persecuted, but not forsaken; struck down, but not destroyed; always carrying about in the body the dying of Jesus, so that the life of Jesus also may be manifested in our body" (2 Cor. 4:8–10). One might be tempted to think that this much suffering would result in a spirit of complaint and bitterness, but such was not the case with Paul.

Instead, he wrote to Timothy, "I thank Christ Jesus our Lord, who has strengthened me, because He considered me faithful, putting me into service" (1 Tim. 1:12). The secret to Paul's strength was his inner reliance on Christ, who had not only called him into the ministry, but also promised to strengthen him to persevere to the end.

A lifestyle of prayer is God's will for every believer in Christ. However, we need to remember that the commands examined in this chapter—rejoice always, give thanks in everything, and pray without ceasing—were first delivered by the Apostle Paul to the *community* of believers in Thessalonica. Therefore, as important as it is for us to stress the value of constant prayer in the life of an individual believer, it is equally significant for us to cultivate the same spirit of God-dependency in our communities of faith, that is, our local churches. God's will includes a desire for churches to demonstrate their reliance upon Him through the cultivation of the discipline of prayer as a tangible part of functioning as the body of Christ. The next seven chapters exemplify the kind of biblical instruction that God's people need to receive on a regular basis in order to develop a healthy theology of prayer.

Part 2
Brief sermons
for prayer
meetings

In order for churches to grow in God-dependency, believers need a regular diet of instruction concerning the discipline of prayer. The Scriptures have so much to say about prayer that it is impossible for any one preacher to exhaust their teaching. Henry Thiessen writes, "No one can read the Bible without being impressed with the large place given to prayer in its pages. Beginning with the conversation between God and Adam, all through the Old Testament and the New there are examples of men who prayed."[1] If a man walks with God for 100 years, he remains a pupil in the school of prayer. In the Scriptures, pastors and elders have an inexhaustible wellspring of biblical teaching to bring to their congregations in fresh, drinkable servings.

Part 2 contains seven chapters comprising brief sermons originally preached as part of whole-church prayer meetings. Each chapter consists of a complete sermon that, when preached, lasts about twenty minutes.

In a one-hour prayer meeting, brief sermons like these provide biblical instruction toward a theology of prayer while at the same time not hindering the primary reason believers gather at a prayer meeting—to pray. The beauty of this approach is that it gives the people of God an opportunity to immediately apply what they have learned from the Scriptures to the practice of God-dependent prayer.

Praying in Jesus's name (John 14:13–14)

Chapter 3

When we pray in the Name of the Lord Jesus, we come the closest to omnipotence that it is possible for mortal man to come.

–William MacDonald

Jesus promises, "Whatever you ask in My name, that will I do, so that the Father may be glorified in the Son. If you ask Me anything in My name, I will do it" (John 14:13–14). In the context of these words, Jesus had just informed His disciples of His approaching departure (vv. 1–15). After He left them, He would build and furnish heaven as their eternal home. He made it clear that His purpose on earth was to glorify His Father, and He faithfully carried this out to the extent that He was able to say to Philip, "He who has seen Me has seen the Father" (v. 9). Jesus then declared that those who believed in Him would do greater works than He had done, by the power of the Holy Spirit whom He promised to send (vv. 12, 16). These works would be accomplished, He said, by praying according to His name.

Here is a radical promise jam-packed with reward. Jesus states that, whatever we ask in His name, He will do it. What does this mean? With a reward like this, why would any of us *not* want to know what Jesus meant? This call to pray in Jesus's name begs us to consider three biblical principles.

Praying in Jesus's name means acknowledging that His death and resurrection have opened prayer's door (v. 6)

In verse 6, Jesus said to Thomas, "I am the way, and the truth, and the life; no one comes to the Father, but through Me." The point is, no one can approach God without repentant faith in Jesus Christ. Without Jesus as our righteous Mediator we are the enemies of God, but through faith in Him we become the children of God. Therefore, Jesus taught His disciples to address

God as "Father." "Pray, then, in this way: 'Our Father who is in heaven'" (Matt. 6:9).

The title "Father" screams relationship—a relationship only made possible through the sacrificial death of Jesus on the cross. In Christ, enemies of God become His friends. In Christ, God's rebels become His followers. In Christ, the devil's children become God's children. Prayer is only possible because the children of God have access to their Father: "through Him we both have our access in one Spirit to the Father" (Eph. 2:18). All sinners alike—whether Jew or Gentile—have access to God through Christ. This is only possible because Jesus tore the veil of the temple in two by offering Himself as both the sacrifice for sin and the High Priest (Matt. 27:51; Heb. 7:27).

According to Hebrews 7:26, Jesus is qualified to be our High Priest because He is "holy, innocent, undefiled, separated from sinners and exalted above the heavens." As our mediator, Jesus offered a sacrifice—Himself. An immediate by-product of His priestly intercession is the access we have to God through prayer.

> Therefore, since we have a great high priest who has passed through the heavens, Jesus the Son of God, let us hold fast our confession. For we do not have a high priest who cannot sympathize with our weaknesses, but One who has been tempted in all things as we are, yet without sin. Therefore let us draw near with confidence to the throne of grace, so that we may receive mercy and find grace to help in time of need.
>
> Heb. 4:14–16

To pray in Jesus's name means we must come to the Father acknowledging that, without the atonement of Christ, God could not and would not ever hear us. It includes a recognition that without being united with Christ we have absolutely no right to utter one word to God. J. C. Ryle provides a fitting illustration: "The bank note without a signature at the bottom is nothing but a worthless piece of paper. The stroke of a pen confers on it all its value. The prayer of a poor child of Adam is a feeble thing in itself, but once endorsed by the hand of the Lord Jesus it availeth much."[1] We may come to God through the merit of our Savior alone since the ink on heaven's "banknote" is the shed blood of Christ.

In light of this, it might do us some good to *begin* praying "in Jesus's name," instead of habitually *ending* our prayers this way. For example, we could say, "Lord, I come to You in Jesus's name. I enter Your presence recognizing that, if it were not for Jesus, my prayers could not be heard at this very moment. I have no righteousness of my own by which I lay claim to Your listening ears. However, I come to You clothed in the righteousness of Jesus." This approach humbles us as it reminds us that our sin was so great that it took the death of the Son of God to satisfy the wrath of the Father against it. Understanding and acknowledging this truth is partially what it means to pray in Jesus's name.

Praying in Jesus's name means praying for that which will bring God the most glory (v. 13)

In John 14:9, Jesus says to Philip, "Have I been so long with you, and yet you have not come to know Me, Philip? He who has seen Me has seen the Father; how can you say, 'Show us the Father'?" Jesus's purpose on earth was to display the glory of God. Jesus is "the image of the invisible God" (Col. 1:15) and is "the radiance of His glory and the exact representation of His nature" (Heb. 1:3).

Everything Jesus did brought glory to God. He consciously deflected glory back to His Father, as He told Philip: "the Father abiding in Me does His works" (John 14:10). Therefore, to do anything "in Jesus's name" is to do it the same way that He would do it. To ask for anything in His name means to ask

47

for what will bring forth the greatest display of God's power. William MacDonald is convinced that "Prayer brings power in our lives and peace to our hearts. When we pray in the Name of the Lord Jesus, we come the closest to omnipotence that it is possible for mortal man to come. Therefore we do ourselves a great disservice when we neglect to pray."[2]

When Scripture speaks of God's name it refers to all that He is—His nature, character, and attributes: what He displays concerning Himself. God's name is all that He is and God's glory is the display of all that He is. Notice how the two are used interchangeably in the following psalms:

> O LORD, our LORD,
>> how majestic is Your name in all the earth,
>> Who have displayed Your splendor [glory] above the heavens!

Ps. 8:1

God's name is majestic. But how do we know this? Because He has displayed it. His glory is what we see, and what we see reveals His name (all that He is) to us.

> Help us, O God of our salvation, for the glory of Your name;
>> And deliver us and forgive our sins for Your name's sake.

Ps. 79:9

The psalmist prayed for God's deliverance so that His glory would be seen by more people—so that His name would be displayed for all to see.

> So the nations will fear the name of the LORD
> And all the kings of the earth Your glory.

Ps. 102:15

Both phrases in the above verse say the same thing, just in two different ways. God's name and His glory are used interchangeably. Consider one more example:

> Let them praise the name of the LORD,
>> For His name alone is exalted;
>
> His glory is above earth and heaven.

Ps. 148:13

We are called to praise the Lord because both His name and His glory are exalted above the heavens and the earth. When we notice the ways in which God makes His presence and power known in our lives and our churches, what should we do? We should praise Him before others so that He receives glory. But what does this mean in relation to the requests we bring to God in prayer?

To pray in Jesus's name means to pray for what will bring Him the most glory. It is to pray, "Lord, in my limited human understanding, this is what I want You to do, but since my knowledge is finite I don't know if this is what will bring You the most glory. Therefore, I pray in Jesus's name—that is, I pray for what will show Your splendor. My desire is that Your answer will be that which will produce an obvious display of Your character to those with whom I have contact."

Remember Jesus's promise: "Whatever you ask in My name, that will I do, so that the Father may be glorified in the Son" (John 14:13). When we find ourselves praying for something that we want, perhaps more than anything we've ever wanted before, can we honestly pray, "Lord, do what will bring you the most glory"? Are we willing to submit to the supremacy of God's glory over our own selfish desires? Whether or not our particular requests agree with His name and His glory, only God might know. However, we need to come to the place where we desire His glory more than our own pleasures (James 4:3).

Praying for that which will bring God the most glory produces two results.

DISPLAYS OF GOD'S GLORY CAUSE HIS CREATURES TO PRAISE HIM (JER. 33:9)

As noted above, God's name and His glory should forever evoke praise from His creatures. In particular, the Old Testament foretold the praise God would receive when Israel and Judah were restored to Him: "'It will be to Me a name of joy, praise and glory before all the nations of the earth which will hear of all the good that I do for them, and they will fear and tremble because of all the good and all the peace that I make for it'" (Jer. 33:9). God does what He does in order to display His glory so that others may see it and benefit from it and praise Him accordingly.

We therefore need to pray, "Lord, I want Your answer to my prayer to cause more people to praise You." This request falls right on the heels of praying for His glory. If we pray for what brings God the most glory it only follows that we also pray for whatever will result in more praise being heaped upon His name. "Through [Jesus] then, let us continually offer up a sacrifice of praise to God, that is, the fruit of lips that give thanks to His name" (Heb. 13:15). What God does in order to reveal His name to us should evoke our praise. This is partially what it means to pray in Jesus's name.

DISPLAYS OF GOD'S GLORY INCLUDE, IN PARTICULAR, DEMONSTRATIONS OF HIS GOODNESS (EXOD. 33:18–19)

In response to Moses' request in Exodus 33:18, "I pray You, show me Your glory!", God said, "I Myself will make all My goodness pass before you, and will proclaim the name of the Lord before you; and I will be gracious to whom I will be gracious, and will show compassion on whom I will show compassion" (Exod. 33:19). God equates His name with His goodness.

For God to show Moses His goodness equaled showing him His name. God's name is not merely a title. It is not a label we tack onto God so that we know what to call Him when we pray. It is His very being, nature, and the sum total of His attributes. To pray in Jesus's name is therefore to desire that others see His goodness, grace, and compassion. It is to be confident that whatever God does for His children will be for His glory and will ultimately display that He is good toward us.

Though our hearts may sometimes doubt the goodness of all that God has brought into our lives, we can rest assured that, according to His wisdom, our heavenly Father only does what is good for us. This is sometimes difficult for us to grasp by faith, but to pray in Jesus's name means to come to the point of saying, "Lord, I don't understand what this trial is all about. I don't comprehend what you are trying to teach me through this suffering, but I do recognize one thing: You are my Father, and You love me and You only do that which is good for me. Therefore, I believe that You will somehow work it together for my good and for Your glory, whether or not I get to understand it in this life" (see Rom. 8:28). This is partially what it means to pray in Jesus's name.

Praying in Jesus's name means praying in submission to His revealed will (vv. 14–15)

Immediately following Jesus's radical promise "If you ask Me anything in My name, I will do it" (John 14:14), He explains, "If you love Me, you will keep My commandments" (v. 15). The revealed will of God is found in the Scriptures, not in our own subjective thoughts or feelings. Jesus makes it clear that if we truly love Him, we will listen to what He says and will do it (see Matt. 7:21–27). However, we do not become, or remain, obedient disciples of Christ by our own power, for Jesus promised divine enablement: "I will ask the Father, and He will give you another Helper, that He may be with you forever" (John 14:16). The Holy Spirit lives within every person who is truly born again (1 Cor. 12:13), and He leads us according to the mind of Christ, which is revealed by the words of the Bible (1 Cor. 2:12–16).

When Jesus returns in all His power and glory, His name will be called "The Word of God" (Rev. 19:13). Jesus is the living Word who has revealed His will in His written Word, which declares His name. This same connection between His name and His Word is seen in the commendation He gave to the church at Sardis: "I know your deeds. Behold, I have put before you an open door which no one can shut, because you have a little power, and have kept My word, and have not denied My name" (Rev. 3:8). To "not deny" is to keep. Therefore, Jesus is saying the same thing in two ways: The church kept His name by keeping His Word, and they kept His Word by not denying His name. As a result of this agreement with Jesus, the church experienced God's power. If God's name is all that He is, and the Word of God is the mind of God in written form (1 Cor. 2:10–16), then the name of God is synonymous with the Word of God. This connection is also made clear in 1 John 5:11–13:

> And the testimony is this, that God has given us eternal life, and this life is in His Son. He who has the Son has the life; he who does not have the Son of God does not have the life. These things I have written to you who believe in the name of the Son of God, so that you may know that you have eternal life.

According to the Apostle John, the person who believes in the "name" of Jesus is the same as the person who believes the "testimony" about Jesus revealed in the Bible. To believe the testimony is to believe Jesus. To believe Jesus is to believe the testimony. Therefore, to pray in Jesus's name is to pray in accordance with His testimony, which is the written Word of God.

This is crucial for us to understand since there is often much subjectivism in the arena of prayer. The believer in Christ can never rightly pray "in Jesus's name" for something that is unbiblical. We cannot pray to God while demanding our own way, ignoring what His Word says, and then add three magical words, "in Jesus's name," thinking we have somehow obligated God to answer us according to our will. Prayer does not change God's mind, but it does change us as He brings our desires into conformity with His will. R. L. Dabney illustrates the truth this way:

> Prayer is not intended to produce a change in God, but in us. Rev. Rowland Hill explained to sailors: "The man in the skiff at the stern of a man-of war, does not pull the ship to himself, in hauling at the line, but pulls the skiff to the ship. This line is prayer. Prayer does not draw God down to us, but draws us up to God, and thus establishes the connection."[3]

It is impossible to stubbornly make demands of God and truly pray in Jesus's name at the same time. To pray in His name means to pray in agreement with who He is and with what He has revealed in His Word. Acceptable prayer flows from a heart that is surrendered to the authority of the Bible.

We have seen what Jesus meant when He made this promise to His disciples: "Whatever you ask in My name, that will I do, so that the Father may be glorified in the Son. If you ask Me anything in My name, I will do it" (John 14:13–14). Jesus meant that the disciples living at that time could ask Him to do anything that would bring His Father glory, and He would do it. But He also meant that future generations of believers could, by the Holy Spirit, ask Him in prayer to do anything that would bring God glory—and honor His name—and He would, and will, do it.

"In Jesus's name" is not a three-word formula attached to the end of our prayers that mechanically secures God's stamp of approval upon our requests. Instead, praying in Jesus's name reflects a person's recognition of God's grace in Christ and the submission of his or her heart (mind, emotions, and will) to the will of God for the glory of God. "In Jesus's name" is not a magical phrase that somehow guarantees that our every prayer will be answered in accordance with our desires. It is an honest, humble acknowledgment that we cannot utter one acceptable word to God without the intercession of Jesus Christ. True prayer is also a heartfelt surrender to God's good and perfect will which leads to the ultimate display of His glory in our lives. This is why Jesus could make the claim that "Whatever you ask in My name, that will I do" (John 14:13). May the Lord truly teach us to pray in Jesus's name!

Praying for unbelievers (John 16:8–11)

... no one can say, "Jesus is Lord," except by the Holy Spirit.

–1 Corinthians 12:3

When it comes to praying for the success of evangelism we sometimes forget the indispensable role of the Holy Spirit in bringing sinners to Christ. It is clear from Scripture that no one can be saved apart from His sovereign work. The Holy Spirit regenerates spiritually dead people, awakening them to God (John 3:5; Titus 3:5). He illuminates Scripture, without which no person can understand divine truth (1 Cor. 2:14). Therefore, we must learn to pray in cooperation with the Holy Spirit's purpose that is predicted by Jesus in John 16:8–11:

> And He, when He comes, will convict the world concerning sin and righteousness and judgment; concerning sin, because they do not believe in Me; and concerning righteousness, because I go to the Father and you no longer see Me; and concerning judgment, because the ruler of this world has been judged.

Jesus promised that the Spirit would convict the world. To *convict* means to convince, to prove, or to bring to realization. The Spirit's work among unbelievers is one of convincing them of truth, that is, of reality as God sees it. The assumption here is that what keeps unbelievers trapped in darkness is the absence of light. The Holy Spirit was sent to bring light to expose the darkness of man's sin and unbelief in order to bring unbelievers to a biblical understanding of three matters: sin, righteousness, and judgment. Knowing the emphasis of the Spirit's work in these three areas helps us understand how best to pray for unbelievers.

The Holy Spirit makes unbelievers aware of their own sinfulness (vv. 8–9)

To pray for unbelievers to receive an awareness of their personal sinfulness means to pray for people to become lost—in the sense of seeing themselves as hopeless without Christ. No one can be saved who has not first seen him- or herself as being in need of salvation. Therefore, we must pray for unbelievers to see their sin just as Isaiah saw his. When Isaiah saw God in His infinite holiness, he knew he was spiritually "ruined" (Isa. 6:5). The holiness of God is the terribly bright searchlight against which even the "smallest" sin looks extremely dirty. Though Isaiah was already a believer when he received the vision, this fresh conviction of his sinfulness illustrates that which it is essential for unbelievers to experience. There will be no firm grasp of Christ as one's sin-bearer without conviction of sin and its ruination—specifically, of the sin of unbelief and its eternal consequences. This Spirit-produced conviction, Jesus says, "[concerns] sin because they do not believe in Me" (John 16:9).

The heart of the gospel is the substitutionary atonement of Christ. Christ died for our sins according to the Scriptures (1 Cor. 15:3). To believe in Christ for salvation means to trust in Him as our own substitute. We must pray for unbelievers to go beyond seeing Jesus as the Savior of the world to seeing Him as their own Savior from their own sin. If people do not see their sin for what it really is—a grave offense against their perfect Creator—how can they direct their faith toward its only acceptable object: the crucified and risen Christ? When unbelievers readily include themselves in the "all" of "all have sinned and fall short of the glory of God" (Rom. 3:23), they are beginning to move toward the experience of salvation.

Therefore, this is how we should pray: *Lord, direct your Holy Spirit to convince _____ of the guilt of his/her sin so that he/she may repent of unbelief and trust the Lord Jesus Christ as his/her substitute on the cross and his/her Savior.*

The Holy Spirit makes unbelievers aware of God's righteousness (v. 10)

To pray for unbelievers to become aware of God's righteousness is to pray that they will understand the reason for the cross. Jesus said that the Spirit would convict "concerning righteousness, because I go to the Father" (John 16:10). Jesus's ascension to the right hand of God is proof that He finished the work He came to do. He willingly allowed His Father to impute the guilt of sinners to Himself so that He might impute His righteousness to us on the basis of faith. "He made Him who knew no sin to be sin on our behalf, so that we might become the righteousness of God in Him" (2 Cor. 5:21).

To pray for awareness of God's righteousness also means to pray for the realization of our own spiritual bankruptcy. Before Saul could be converted he had to be brought to the point of accepting that all his righteous deeds were as filthy rags (Isa. 64:6) and then of counting every item on his spiritual résumé as "rubbish" in order that he might "gain Christ" (Phil. 3:8). Only then could he be found in Christ, "not having a righteousness of [his] own derived from the Law, but that which is through faith in Christ, the righteousness which comes from God on the basis of faith" (Phil. 3:9).

Therefore, this is how we should pray: *Lord, unleash the power of your Spirit upon _____ so that he/she will become aware of his/her spiritual bankruptcy and desperate need of the righteousness of Christ, which can only be received by faith.*

The Holy Spirit makes unbelievers aware of God's future judgment (v. 11)

To pray for awareness of judgment is to pray that unbelievers will see the urgency of their need to repent. Knowledge of judgment is intended to compel sinners to cry out to God for the forgiveness their guilty consciences are convinced they need. Scriptural statements such as that found in Hebrews 9:27—"inasmuch as it is appointed for men to die once and after this comes judgment"—are meant to move sinners off dead center and send them searching for pardon.

The Spirit convicts the world of judgment "because the ruler of this world has been judged" (John 16:11). This is a reference to the cross, which was yet future when Jesus spoke these words predicting Satan's defeat. Hebrews 2:14 assures us that through His death, Jesus rendered "powerless him who had the power of death, that is, the devil." The judgment Jesus referred to is that which is related to His work on the cross. Not only was Satan defeated there, but sin was judged at Calvary, too. Each sinner must now come to grips with the atonement Jesus provided in order to purchase redemption. The future judgment that awaits all sinners will be based on whether or not they have applied the finished work of Christ to their own spiritual needs. An awareness of this coming judgment is a divinely sent conviction that moves sinners toward conversion.

Therefore, this is how we should pray: *Lord, move your Spirit to convince _____ that, apart from repentant faith in Christ, his/her sin of unbelief will lead him/her to condemnation on Judgment Day. Please cause the Spirit to compel him/her to flee to Christ for safety.*

No one can be saved apart from the Holy Spirit's convicting work: "… no one can say, 'Jesus is Lord,' except by the Holy Spirit" (1 Cor. 12:3). The Spirit's tool to bring about this conviction is the Word of God, which is able to convict of sin and to give birth to saving faith (Heb. 4:12; Rom. 10:17). Therefore, a commitment to pray in cooperation with the Spirit demands that we also do everything in our power to expose unbelievers to the truth of the gospel. We must get beyond praying, "Lord, help so and so to get saved." We must expose people to the Word of truth and then pray for the Spirit to complete the work of conviction that Jesus promised. Then, and only then, will His convincing power be unleashed upon the minds and hearts of our unsaved loved ones, friends, and neighbors in order that they may be brought to Jesus.

Praying for government leaders (1 Tim. 2:1–4)

Chapter 5

The wonder of today's church is that so much goes on with so little praying.

–Alex Montoya

How do national and civil leaders bear up under the enormous pressures they face every day? How do they continue to perform their appointed tasks without being crippled by weariness? How do they maintain their composure as they become dartboards for honest critics as well as false accusers? One answer is found in a church's ministry of prayer.

When we commit to praying for our leaders (whether or not we agree with them), God is pleased with us and is pleased to work in their hearts according to His will. In relation to this divinely given duty, one passage in particular contains fundamental principles every believer needs to understand.

> First of all, then, I urge that entreaties and prayers, petitions and thanksgivings, be made on behalf of all men, for kings and all who are in authority, so that we may lead a tranquil and quiet life in all godliness and dignity. This is good and acceptable in the sight of God our Savior, who desires all men to be saved and to come to the knowledge of the truth.
>
> 1 Tim. 2:1–4

In these verses we hear the apostle's plea to us to be obedient to God by praying for our leaders.

The priority (v. 1a)

Paul begins his exhortation with a phrase that calls attention to the primacy of prayer in the life of the church. "First of all" is a plea to keep first things first. It is an appeal not only to individual Christians, but, since the book was originally written to instruct Timothy concerning local church life (3:15), it is a call to churches and their leaders to place utmost importance on prayer and thereby lead by example. As a pastor, Timothy needed to guard against prayer being openly abandoned by members of his flock or subtly replaced by self-reliance in the body life of his church.

One of the "secrets" of the power of the New Testament church (though it is laid open for all to see) is prayer, plain and simple. Acts 4:31 reveals one example: "when they had prayed, the place where they had gathered together was shaken, and they were all filled with the Holy Spirit and began to speak the word of God with boldness." Prayer unleashes the Spirit's power in the church. Prayer must therefore be maintained as a high priority in the life of the church.

I am convinced our churches will not experience the fullness of the Spirit's power until we return to the priority of prayer, not only as individual believers who pray in private, but also as churches filled with people who cry out to God *together*. Alex Montoya agrees: "The wonder of today's church is that so much goes on with so little praying. The answer to many churches' problems is not more seminars, programs, and promotional gimmicks but more intercession on the part of God's people, both as a group and in the closet."[1] It is therefore essential for us to listen to the apostolic plea to churches to be committed to prayer.

The plea (vv. 1b–2a)

"I urge" is a strong plea carrying the meaning of "coming alongside in order to exhort." The same word is used in Romans 12:1: "I *urge* you, brethren, by the mercies of God, to present your bodies a living and holy sacrifice, acceptable to God, which is your spiritual service of worship." Even though Paul possessed apostolic authority to command Timothy, he chose instead to make a strong appeal to him to recognize the irreplaceable priority of prayer.

Paul used four different words to paint a balanced picture of prayer. "Entreaties" refers to prayers prompted by the awareness of needs. "Prayers" is a general term referring to approaching God with reverence. "Petitions" are compassionate prayers generated from empathy with others. "Thanksgivings" are specific praises to God for the works that He has done. The apostolic appeal is general at first and then gets specific. With these words, Paul provides a sampling of prayers that should be made on behalf of "all men," but especially "for kings and all who are in authority" (vv. 1–2).

The purpose (vv. 2b–4)

"[S]o that" is a clear statement of purpose. The purpose of praying for our government leaders is threefold.

To promote peaceful and godly living (v. 2)

First, we must pray so that "we may lead a tranquil and quiet life in all godliness and dignity." This refers to an external as well as an inner peace. How does praying for our leaders promote peace? Praying for God to give our leaders wisdom in world affairs may promote peaceful living, as will praying for the writing of good laws that honor biblical principles. According to Proverbs 21:1, "The king's heart is like channels of water in the hand of the Lord; He turns it wherever He wishes." If we really believe this truth, we will get down on our knees in order to lift our government leaders before God in prayer. We must ask God to lead them like water in His hand to craft righteous laws. We should pray for God-fearing legislators to be given "moral antennas" to discern corrupt statutes as they move through the lawmaking process so that they may oppose them and we may live in "godliness and dignity."

Godliness includes our holy attitudes and conduct toward God. It is much more than outward conformity to a list of dos and don'ts. As performance-driven sinners, we are often able to meet up to man's standards while still possessing heart attitudes that are disgusting to God. Godliness is first an inner quality, but in time it works itself out in our behavior. *Dignity* refers to gravity or moral earnestness. It is a heavy word that emphasizes the seriousness of the matter. Godly living is serious business. Let us therefore pray for those in high positions of authority in our cities and our country.

To please God (v. 3)

Second, we must pray for our government leaders because it is "good and acceptable in the sight of God our Savior." It pleases God, which ought to be the top priority of our lives. Matthew 6:33 calls us to this motive for life: "seek first His kingdom and His righteousness; and all these things will be added to you." When we have this overarching philosophy of life, all peripheral matters fall into their proper place in their proper time. "Set your mind on the things above, not on the things that are on earth" (Col. 3:2).

This was the Apostle Paul's priority: "Therefore we also have as our ambition, whether at home or absent, to be pleasing to Him" (2 Cor. 5:9). Whether alive or dead, Paul's ambition was to please God. Do we have the same ambition? Paul prayed for the Colossian believers to be "filled with the knowledge of His will in all spiritual wisdom and understanding, so that you will walk in a manner worthy of the Lord, *to please Him* in all respects" (Col. 1:9–10). One clear way to please God is by faithfully praying for our government leaders.

To propagate the gospel (v. 4)

Third, we must pray for our government leaders because God "desires all men to be saved." Conversion takes place when sinners "come to the knowledge of the truth." Therefore, we must pray for the souls of our civil leaders, that they will come to know Jesus Christ as the Way, the Truth, and the Life (John 14:6). We should pray for the Holy Spirit's convicting work

(John 16:8), for faithful witnesses to be heard (Rom. 10:14), and for the faith-giving power of the Word of God (Rom. 10:17).

Our government leaders need us. They need us to pray for them with all diligence. This obedient habit pleases God, but is also a means of making a difference for the sake of righteousness in our world and for the sake of the gospel for all eternity.

Praying with a forgiving heart (Matt. 6:12–15)

Chapter 6

The person who will not forgive had better hope that he will never sin.

–Lehman Straus

If we have ever been overcome by the guilt of our sin, we can relate to King David's expression of the freedom of forgiveness: "How blessed is he whose transgression is forgiven, whose sin is covered!" (Ps. 32:1). If God were to openly parade our sin before others, who among us would not want to crawl under a rock and hide forever? To be forgiven is to be free from the bondage of sin's debt and the fear of its punishment. The Bible contains much joyful testimony praising God for His forgiveness.

> Bless the LORD, O my soul,
> And forget none of His benefits;
> Who pardons all your iniquities;
> Who heals all your diseases.
>
> Ps. 103:2–3

> The LORD is compassionate and gracious,
> Slow to anger and abounding in lovingkindness.
> He will not always strive with us,
> Nor will He keep His anger forever.
> He has not dealt with us according to our sins,
> Nor rewarded us according to our iniquities.
> For as high as the heavens are above the earth,
> So great is His lovingkindness toward those who fear
> Him.
> As far as the east is from the west,
> So far has He removed our transgressions from us.
>
> Ps. 103:8–12

> Who is a God like You, who pardons iniquity

> And passes over the rebellious act of the remnant of
> His possession?
> He does not retain His anger forever,
> Because He delights in unchanging love.
> He will again have compassion on us;
> He will tread our iniquities under foot.
> Yes, You will cast all their sins
> Into the depths of the sea.

Micah 7:18–19

> But He, being compassionate, forgave their iniquity
> and did not destroy them;
> And often He restrained His anger
> And did not arouse all His wrath.
> Thus He remembered that they were but flesh,
> A wind that passes and does not return.

Ps. 78:38–39

Since Jesus taught that a heart that has been forgiven much loves much (Luke 7:47), our thinking will be affected by how often we meditate on God's forgiveness of us in Jesus Christ. If we regularly ponder the depth of our own sinfulness, like the woman who washed Jesus's feet with her tears, and consider the greater depth of God's forgiveness, we will grow in our love for Him. It is when we forget God's benefits that our hearts become proud. If we are not careful, we who have been forgiven much can act like those who think they have been forgiven little and, consequently, become slow to forgive others who sin against us. When this happens the soil of our hearts is in danger of being loosened and fertilized for the root of bitterness to grow. We must therefore consciously practice forgiveness. If we do not, a spirit of unforgiveness will most certainly destroy the effectiveness of our prayer lives.

Jesus taught the importance of forgiveness and how it relates to prayer in what is often called "The Lord's Prayer." Let's think on the portions of this model prayer that relate to the principle of forgiveness.

> [Pray in this way] And forgive us our debts, as we also have forgiven our debtors ... For if you forgive others for their transgressions, your heavenly Father will also forgive you. But if you do not forgive others, then your Father will not forgive your transgressions.

> Matt. 6:12, 14–15

Here we learn three characteristics of a forgiving heart and its effects upon prayer. By application, we also learn how the enemy of pride fights against the obedient practice of forgiveness.

A forgiving heart is energized by a healthy awareness of personal sin (v. 12a)

In His model prayer, Jesus includes confession of sin as a necessary element of God-dependent prayer. We ought to pray, "forgive us our debts." A daily awareness of our own sinfulness will lead us to regularly ask God for His forgiveness, which is a healthy part of the process of spiritual growth. It is when we remember that we ourselves are wretched that we will in turn praise God for the victory found only in Jesus Christ (Rom. 7:24–25).

PRIDE IS THE ENEMY OF A FORGIVING HEART

Unforgiving people (those with bitter hearts) think themselves superior to others. Their shallow recognition of their own depravity makes it difficult for them to imagine that they themselves are quite capable of committing the very sins for which they stubbornly refuse to forgive their brothers and sisters. Unforgiving people have not lately thought about the profundity of their own sin.

In contrast, those with forgiving hearts humbly acknowledge

their own need for a daily supply of God's grace and mercy. As a result, they are trained to be ready to forgive others.

A forgiving heart is expected of the one who is forgiven (v. 12b)

Jesus continues, "as we also have forgiven our debtors." Oh, the power of that little word "as"! Jesus assumed that forgiving others would be the general practice of the child of God. The Bible expects Christians to be forgiving people. In fact, it entertains no other healthy option. We are called to the highest standard of practicing forgiveness. We are called to forgive *as* God forgives: "Be kind to one another, tender-hearted, forgiving each other, *just as* God in Christ also has forgiven you" (Eph. 4:32, emphasis added; see also Col. 3:13).

PRIDE IS THE ENEMY OF A FORGIVING HEART

Unforgiving people (those with bitter hearts) have been deceived into thinking that somehow they deserve forgiveness, but their offenders do not. Why else would they be so reluctant to freely grant it? Unforgiving people have short memories concerning their own sin. Pride has erased their remembrance and they have forgotten the blackness of their own sin. Pride has blinded the eyes of their hearts so that they no longer see the ugliness of their own past. They fail to remember the depth of the grace and forgiveness that God has so freely bestowed upon them and therefore are slow to pass them on to others.

In contrast, those with forgiving hearts have a long memory concerning their own sin, but a short memory concerning the sins of others. The long-lasting memory of their own sin is grievous, but the remembrance produces joy as their hearts reflect on the new-found freedom of forgiveness in Jesus. Equal joy fills their hearts when humble people are able to extend that same forgiveness to others who have sinned against them.

A forgiving heart secures its own forgiveness and God's listening ear (vv. 14–15)

Jesus places a sobering, if not frightening, condition upon our own forgiveness. If we forgive, "[our] heavenly Father will also forgive [us]." If we refuse to forgive others, "[our] Father will not forgive [our] transgressions." This means that bitterness (a refusal to forgive) breaks our fellowship with God. Since God refuses to forgive those who refuse to forgive others, we may conclude that God does not listen to the prayers of bitter Christians. As Lehman Straus has written, "The person who will not forgive had better hope that he will never sin."[1]

PRIDE IS THE ENEMY OF A FORGIVING HEART

Unforgiving people (those with bitter hearts) refuse to release their brothers and sisters from sin's debt because they have exalted themselves to be their judges. As judges, they will execute whatever punishment they think is necessary until their offenders "prove" they are worthy of their forgiveness.

In contrast, those with forgiving hearts leave vengeance in the hands of the Lord (Rom. 12:19). Forgiving people have no desire to get even because they know God has already got even with sin at the cross.

Whether or not we are forgiving people will greatly influence the effectiveness of our prayers. If we have a daily awareness of our own sinfulness we will more readily fulfill our Christian responsibility to practice forgiveness toward those who repent of their sins against us. As a result, we will please God, guard our own hearts from bitterness, and live in the true freedom of forgiveness.

Calling for your elders (James 5:13–18)

Chapter 7

It is a wise man of very old time who in one breath
bids us look to the physician with his remedies and
to the Lord who is behind the physician and works
in and through him and his remedies.

–Benjamin B. Warfield

James 5:13–18 is a passage of Scripture that is too often
misunderstood in our churches. Perhaps that is because we
have not taken time to consider its teaching.

> Is anyone among you suffering? Then he must pray. Is
> anyone cheerful? He is to sing praises. Is anyone among
> you sick? Then he must call for the elders of the church
> and they are to pray over him, anointing him with oil in
> the name of the Lord; and the prayer offered in faith will
> restore the one who is sick, and the Lord will raise him
> up, and if he has committed sins, they will be forgiven
> him. Therefore, confess your sins to one another, and
> pray for one another so that you may be healed. The
> effective prayer of a righteous man can accomplish
> much. Elijah was a man with a nature like ours, and he
> prayed earnestly that it would not rain, and it did not
> rain on the earth for three years and six months. Then
> he prayed again, and the sky poured rain and the earth
> produced its fruit.

The main theme of the passage is the place and power of prayer
in the life of the suffering believer. Every verse in the paragraph
contains an explicit reference to prayer. James insists that the
Christian life find its focal point in a vital relationship with
God in prayer. Oswald Sanders writes of prayer, "It touches
infinite extremes, for it is at once the simplest form of speech
that infant lips can try and the sublimest strains that reach the
majesty on High. It is indeed the Christian's vital breath and

native air."[1] Clearly, prayer is the most obvious expression of God-dependency.

Prayer, however, is not merely something James preached about. He lived it. According to church history, this apostle spent so much time in prayer that his knees became as hard as those of a camel. As "Old Camel-Knees" provides instruction concerning the ministry of prayer, he makes it clear that one of the specific ways in which church members show their dependence upon God is by calling on their church shepherds when they are in need of intercession.

Here we see three exhortations to believers in various circumstances, three expectations of the focused ministry of the elders toward the sick, and one example of a righteous man who accomplished much through prayer. Specific instruction concerns the unique intercession that pastors and elders may carry out on behalf of their sheep.

Three exhortations (vv. 13–14)

Believers are exhorted to demonstrate living faith by turning to God in the midst of the diverse experiences of life. Three different kinds of people are addressed here: the suffering, the smiling, and the sick.

THE SUFFERING SHOULD PRAY (V. 13A)

"[H]e must pray" is a continual command meaning, "Keep on praying always." It should be our habit to turn to God in prayer in times of suffering and emotional distress. We *ourselves* should pray for ourselves when we are suffering. J. C. Ryle exhorts,

> Just as it is with the mind and body, so it is with the soul. There are certain things absolutely needful to the soul's health and well-being. Each must attend to these things for himself. Each must repent for himself. Each must apply to Christ for himself. And for himself each must

speak to God and pray. You must do it for yourself, for by nobody else can it be done.[2]

Of course, the command to pray for ourselves does not prohibit asking others to pray for us, which is important and necessary as well (1 Thes. 5:25; 2 Thes. 3:1). However, too many believers are quick to add requests to their church's prayer list but neglect participation in the prayer meetings themselves. They want *others* to pray for them and for their loved ones, but they do not want to pray themselves. If a need is not great enough for a person to pray for him- or herself, then perhaps it is not important enough for the whole church to pray either. James says, "If anyone is suffering, he *must* pray."

Suffering encourages prayer. This is one of the points James makes at the beginning of his book:

> Consider it all joy, my brethren, when you encounter various trials, knowing that the testing of your faith produces endurance. And let endurance have its perfect result, so that you may be perfect and complete, lacking in nothing. But if any of you lacks wisdom, let him ask of God, who gives to all generously and without reproach, and it will be given to him. But he must ask in faith without any doubting, for the one who doubts is like the surf of the sea, driven and tossed by the wind. For that man ought not to expect that he will receive anything from the Lord, being a double-minded man, unstable in all his ways.
>
> 1:2–8

Suffering has the unique power to drive us to our knees in order that we may seek the wisdom needed to discern how we should respond in our time of trial.

The smiling should sing (v. 13b)

Those who have an attitude of cheerfulness should "sing

praises." The word translated "sing" originally meant "to play a stringed instrument," but it can also be translated "glorify God" (see Rom 15:9). This praise is a conscious choice involving the mind and heart. Paul writes in 1 Corinthians 14:15, "I will pray with the spirit and I will pray with the mind also; I will sing with the spirit and I will sing with the mind also."

When Christians are filled with the Holy Spirit and the Word of God, we will sing and make melody in our hearts to the Lord (Eph. 5:19; Col. 3:16). A quick comparison of Ephesians 5:18–19 with Colossians 3:16 yields an important biblical principle: To be filled with the Holy Spirit primarily means to be filled with the Word of God. The filling of the Spirit is not mystical, but immensely practical. To live under the Spirit's control is to live in submission to the book that He inspired (2 Tim. 3:16–17; 2 Peter 1:19–21).

THE SICK SHOULD CALL (V. 14)

The balance and bulk of our passage (James 5:13–18) addresses those who are "sick," that is, those without strength. This word refers to bodily weakness, but may denote any kind of weakness, mental, moral, or spiritual. The word is also used to refer to weak faith or a weak conscience. It may more literally be translated as "weary." Those who are sick are instructed to "call for the elders" to come and pray with them. Notice that the initiative is placed on the sick person to "call," that is, call for him- or herself, if possible. In the case of a person who is timid, taking this action may need to be encouraged (1 Thes. 5:14). The elders are then to go to the sick person to pray over him or her. "Pray" is the central verb, the specific activity of the elders. "Anointing" is a participle, an activity secondary to praying.

The oil referred to here is simple olive oil, the common oil used to show honor to guests, rather than ceremonial oil. This oil was also used medicinally. In this context the oil probably both refers to the use of medicine and symbolizes the presence of the Spirit and the healing power of God. Certainly God would not have us ignore His abundant provision of help through medicine and doctors, but He also would not have us place our faith wholly in them.[3] Benjamin B. Warfield, a theologian at Princeton in the late 1800s and early 1900s, encouraged this balanced understanding:

> The emphasis falls not on the anointing, but on its being done "in the name of the Lord," and the whole becomes an exhortation to Christians, when they are sick, to seek unto the Lord as well as to their physician … God has very much to do with the cures wrought by the surgeon's knife or the physician's medicaments; so much to do with them that it is He who really makes them. It is to Him that the efficacy of all means is due, in general and in particular. It is a wise man of very old time who in one breath bids us look to the physician with his remedies and to the Lord who is behind the physician and works in and through him and his remedies.[4]

It is significant to note that James did not regard the oil as the healing agent or the anointing as possessing some kind of magical power, but it is "the prayer offered in faith" that heals. This anticipates certain results.

Three expectations (vv. 15–16)

Praying in faith includes the anticipation that God will hear and answer. J. C. Ryle writes, "… we should cultivate the habit of expecting answers to our prayers. We should do like the merchant who sends his ships to sea. We should not be satisfied, unless we see some return."[5] We must pray with expectation. Specifically, James mentions three results of the prayer of faith.

Restoration (v. 15)

First, the troubled believer who has called for the elders can expect to be restored. "The prayer," a specific prayer—a strong, fervent wish that is offered in faith—will be the agent of restoration. God in His sovereignty has ordained that some things He has already determined to do will only be accomplished as a result of prayer. Iain Murray says it well when he writes, "God has chosen to make prayer a *means* of blessing, not so that the fulfilment of his purposes becomes dependent upon us, but rather to help us learn *our* absolute dependence upon him."[6] If God wills it so, the restoration that James speaks of may indeed be physical, as the elders have prayed. However, it may be that God's purpose in ordaining sickness is to get the sick person's attention in order to accomplish a more important spiritual work in his or her soul, which the next phrase suggests.

REPENTANCE (VV. 15–16)

Second, if spiritual healing alone is what God has in mind, He will use the physical suffering of the one who is sick to open his or her spiritual eyes, resulting in genuine brokenness of spirit and confession of sins. As a result, those specific sins "will be forgiven." From this text we are right to conclude that sickness may be the result of personal sin. However, this is not *always* the case. Jesus made this clear in his response to His disciples' question, "'Rabbi, who sinned, this man or his parents, that he would be born blind?' Jesus answered, 'It was neither that this man sinned, nor his parents; but it was so that the works of God might be displayed in him'" (John 9:1–3). Sickness is sometimes completely unrelated to personal sin. But, as is made clear by James, sometimes our sickness is the direct result of our sin.

This certainly was the case in the church at Corinth. The reason why Paul instructed the believers to examine themselves before they partook of the Lord's Supper was because there were obvious sins in the church, which, for some who were unrepentant, resulted in sickness and death. "But a man must examine himself, and in so doing he is to eat of the bread and drink of the cup. For he who eats and drinks, eats and drinks judgment to himself if he does not judge the body rightly. For this reason many among you are weak and sick, and a number sleep. But if we judged ourselves rightly, we would not be judged" (1 Cor. 11:28–31). Here is a clear example of sickness, even unto death, as the consequence of personal sin. Since sickness is sometimes the result of personal sin, the sick person who has called for the elders should take time to examine his or her own heart and life, asking God to expose any hidden sin (in the spirit of Ps. 139:23–24), in order that he or she may confess it to God and to the church shepherds.

James instructs the one who is sick to "confess" his or her sins. The word *confess* refers to an open or full confession of "sins," that is, specific sins that God has brought to mind. This implies that confession of sin is another reason to call the elders and is sure evidence of humility and a desire to be restored to fellowship with God. Hiebert writes, "Unconfessed sins have an upward as well as outward impact on the life of a believer. Such sins block the pathway of prayer to God and hinder interpersonal relations. Confession of sin is a Christian duty and a powerful deterrent to sin."[7] When biblical confession takes place, the repentant one "may be healed." Perhaps God, in response to the prayer of the elders, will choose to provide both physical and spiritual restoration.

Righteousness (v. 16)

Third, the sick person's repentance, which is demonstrated by honest confession, yields a practical righteousness. The "righteous man" that James speaks of is not a man who does not sin (there is none but the God-man, Jesus Christ), but it is the one who, when he has sinned, honestly and humbly deals with the offense before God, and others if necessary. The righteous person is the one who stands in a right relationship with God through faith in Christ and lives out the reality of authentic faith.

When this kind of person prays, his or her prayers "accomplish much"; that is, they work on his or her behalf. In contrast, the person who cherishes unrighteousness will not see powerful answers to prayer. Unconfessed sin, as admitted by the psalmist, is a barrier to answered prayer: "If I regard wickedness in my heart, the Lord will not hear" (Ps. 66:18).

One example (vv. 17–18)

James concludes this description of the unique prayer ministry of church elders by providing an historical example to whom his readers can relate—the praying prophet Elijah. Three characteristics of this man of prayer are mentioned in the text.

ELIJAH WAS ONE OF US (V. 17A)

Though he is a famous Bible character, Elijah was "a man with a nature like ours." He was a sinner like us. He was not some kind of super-saint. Elijah was just a man. "The Bible records that he suffered the same human weaknesses that we do: he became hungry (1 Kings 17:11), afraid (1 Kings 19:3), and depressed (1 Kings 19:9–14)."[8] He battled the same sin-nature and resisted the temptations we all have in common (1 Cor. 10:13). But he was also a man of faith who believed that God could do what seemed impossible.

ELIJAH PRAYED EARNESTLY (V. 17)

Elijah therefore prayed "earnestly," which literally means "he prayed with prayer." Elijah did not pray halfheartedly. Instead, he prayed with a whole heart that was devoted to God. Charles Spurgeon once said, "Without the heart prayer is a wretched mockery. There is as much grace in the bark of a dog or the grunt of a swine as in a form of prayer if the heart be absent … God is as likely to hear the cry of ravens than to regard prayers uttered in chapels or churches, if the mind is not in earnest."[9] Like the prophet Elijah, we are called to cultivate a heart that is earnestly "devoted to prayer" (Rom. 12:12).

Elijah reaped the fruit of his prayers (vv. 17–18)

How Elijah prayed is how God answered. He prayed for no rain and the land was dry for three-and-a-half years. He prayed again, this time for rain, and a great cloud burst open (see 1 Kings 17:1–7; 18:1). So will it be for the men and women of God who will trust God enough to cry out to Him.

If our faith is authentic, we will pray. We will pray when we are suffering trials. We will pray when life is good. And we will pray when we are sick and in distress. When sickness or spiritual weakness lays hold of us in a severe way, God provides a remedy through the prayerful ministry of church shepherds. The church is a body. When one part suffers the whole body feels the effects. Therefore, it is important for believers who are battling ongoing physical sickness to consider these words from James and act accordingly. We must not be too proud to ask our spiritual leaders to pray for us. But we must approach prayer with God-dependent faith, repentance, and a willingness to change our ways. We must approach the heavenly throne with faith in God as our Healer and repentance toward God our Father, who loves us enough to chasten us when we sin and to use our suffering to stimulate our growth in grace.

How husbands get their prayers answered (1 Peter 3:7)

To take the time to maintain a good marriage is God's will; it is serving God; it is a spiritual activity pleasing in His sight.

–Wayne Grudem

This is the most convicting message *for me*—since, as a husband and father, I have innumerable prayers that I want God to answer. A number of years ago, while wondering why so many of my prayers seemed to bounce off the ceiling, I voiced my confusion to God in prayer just as David did: "How long, O Lord? Will you forget me forever? How long will You hide Your face from me?" (Ps. 13:1). And I confessed, "I am weary with my crying; my throat is parched; my eyes fail while I wait for my God" (Ps. 69:3). Graciously, God answered my anxious queries through means of gentle correction from His Word. One morning, as I read through Peter's first letter, God clearly spoke to my heart and revealed the reason for His silence:

> You husbands in the same way, live with your wives in an understanding way, as with someone weaker, since she is a woman; and show her honor as a fellow heir of the grace of life, so that your prayers will not be hindered.

> 1 Peter 3:7

The phrase "so that your prayers will not be hindered" pierced my heart. Further study revealed that the word translated "hindered" also means "to cut in on, to interrupt." It was at that moment I realized my prayers were being interrupted by my self-centeredness and consequent need to grow in the practice of what it means to truly honor my wife. My disobedience was interrupting my prayers in the same way my children sometimes interrupt me. This became a life-changing insight. As a result, I thanked God for opening my eyes, confessed my sins to Him, and asked Him to change my heart to reflect the servanthood of Jesus (Phil. 2:1–4).

First Peter 3:7 reveals a weighty principle: A person's relationship with God is affected by his or her relationship with others. As believers, we are usually aware of the opposite truth—a believer's relationship with God affects his or her relationship with others. However, we often fail to see how our horizontal relationships with people do affect our vertical relationship with God (see Matt. 5:28). In this case, the effectiveness of a husband's prayer life is greatly determined by the manner in which he cares for his wife. Peter begins the verse, "You husbands in the same way," which links this exhortation to the previous ones in which Peter calls citizens to be submissive to their governments (2:13–17), servants to their masters (2:18), and wives to their unsaved, or disobedient, husbands (3:1–6), each of which should be motivated by a desire to flesh out the gospel by following the submissive example of Christ (2:19–25).

The verse under consideration in this chapter is a call to husbands to submit to God by treating their wives as God would have them treated. Here is a call to husbands to practice considerate leadership. The warning about hindered prayer serves, then, as the divine means of motivating husbands to obey God's command. There are two aspects to this command.

God answers the prayers of husbands who *understand* their wives (v. 7a)

To live with your wife "in an understanding way" means to dwell with her according to knowledge and consideration. The word translated "understanding" is *gnosis*, which can refer to Christian insight as well as tact. This is a command, a clarion call to every Christian husband to know and understand his wife. For a husband to live with his wife in ignorance is to continue to live in disobedience to God. Therefore, husbands should seize every opportunity they are given to become more knowledgeable about their wives. This knowledge "consists not in intellectual superiority, but in understanding sympathy and respect for the weak."[1] Clearly, then, a heart of understanding is what is in view.

The basis for this command to the husband is that his wife is "someone weaker." She is weaker emotionally and physically, not morally, spiritually, or intellectually. It is obvious that women do not possess the same natural brawn as men and therefore require consideration and gentleness, being more vulnerable. Kenneth Wuest explains the meaning of the phrase "someone weaker," which in some translations is rendered "weaker vessel":

> The word "vessel" is the translation of a Greek word referring to a vessel used in the services of the temple (Mark 11:16), also to household utensils. The English word comes from a Latin word *vassellum*, the diminutive form of *vas*, a vase, the Latin words referring to a receptacle which covers and contains. Thus, the word comes to refer to an instrument whereby something is accomplished. It is used in the latter sense here. The word is used of Paul who is called "a chosen vessel" (Acts 9:15), a chosen instrument of God. The husband is to dwell with the wife, remembering that she is an instrument of God as well as the husband, a child of God to be used by Him to His glory. The husband must ever keep in mind that she is the weaker instrument of the two, not morally or intellectually, but physically. This attitude toward the wife on the part of the husband therefore includes loving consideration of the wife in view of the fact that she is not physically as strong as he is.[2]

A Christian husband must recognize the physical limitations of the female gender and, therefore, must not expect his wife to do the same as that which is expected of a man. As domestic abuse pervades our world, this command clearly rules out any form of rough handling. God does not listen to husbands who "manhandle" their wives.

Allow me to offer some other practical applications of this command.

- A husband must understand his wife's uniqueness. She is like all other women, and yet she is not. A husband must seek to know this unique creation whom God has made to be his helper (Gen. 2:18).

- A husband must respect his wife as a weaker vessel and provide her with security, stability, and strong leadership. It is a cop-out for a Christian husband to claim that his wife should get her security from the Lord. Although that to an extent is true, the husband must come to accept that he is the primary means God has ordained to provide earthly security and stability for his wife. This is not sinful dependence on the wife's part; God has made her to be reliant upon her husband. It is therefore her husband's duty before God to care for her (1 Tim. 5:8; Eph. 5:28–30).

- A husband must protect his wife since she is more vulnerable than he. Women are fragile and, like an expensive vase, must be handled with care. A husband must consciously avoid putting his wife under excessive physical, emotional, or financial stress if it is within his power to do so (Eph. 5:28–29).

God answers the prayers of husbands who *honor* their wives (v. 7b)

In the culture of Peter's day, women were considered inferior to men. For that reason, Peter's command was a bold challenge to the unbiblical mindset that husbands of his day had perhaps unknowingly adopted. Instead of treating their wives as second-class citizens, husbands are here commanded to grant them "honor." *Honor* is the same word translated "precious" in 1 Peter 1:19. To honor means to hold in high regard due to recognition of another person's value or worth. Wuest says, "Husbands should keep a special place of honor in their hearts for their wives. They should treat them with special deference, courtesy, respect, and kindness."[3] Unfortunately, in our day, too many husbands take better care of their automobiles than they do their wives. My brethren, this ought not to be!

A believing wife is to be treated "as a fellow heir of the grace of life." A Christian husband must remember that his wife is equal in value and status before God. Christ died for her just as He died for him. Galatians 3:28 teaches, "There is neither Jew nor Greek, there is neither slave nor free man, there is neither male nor female; for you are all one in Christ Jesus." This truth does not eliminate the husband's headship or the distinct God-given role of the wife as the husband's supportive helper, but rather stresses the fact that all superficial distinctions have been removed with regard to inheriting salvation. All must come to God by faith in Christ, regardless of birth, gender, or social status. As a result of this principle, the Christian husband must not treat his wife as if she is spiritually inferior to him, for she is not.

Allow me to offer some simple applications of this command.

- A husband must hold his wife in high esteem, as one who is precious. He must treat her as his most valuable "possession" and consider her more important than himself (Phil. 2:3).
- A husband must show his wife courtesy, kindness, and consideration. He must speak kind and thoughtful words to her and perform courteous actions toward her. He must not take her love for granted and thus treat her rudely (1 Cor. 13:5).

- A husband must listen to, value, and prayerfully evaluate his wife's counsel. God gave Eve to Adam as his "helper" (Gen. 2:18). A husband who stubbornly plows ahead with his own plans without listening to the wise counsel of his wife is foolish.
- A husband must treat his wife with gentleness. If there are times when he must speak firmly, he must do so with wisdom, not harshness (James 3:13).
- A husband must cherish his wife and give her faithful attention. She should know she is the only woman who holds his interest. Proverbs 18:22 says, "He who finds a wife finds a good thing, and obtains favor from the Lord."
- A husband must not belittle or depreciate his wife. He must not treat her, or speak to her, with an air of superiority (Col. 3:12). Instead, he should be thankful for her and communicate that appreciation in creative ways.
- A husband must serve his wife in small and big ways that communicate love. A Christian husband must not treat his wife like a household slave. He should model biblical servanthood by helping her with the housework and the care of their children (Mark 10:45).

What is the motivation for a Christian husband to treat his wife in this way? That his "prayers will not be hindered." Wayne Grudem explains,

> This hindering of prayers is a form of God's fatherly discipline, which Hebrews 12:3–11 reminds us is for our good and is given to those whom God loves. So concerned is God that Christian husbands live in an understanding and loving way with their wives that He interrupts His relationship with them when they do not do so! No Christian husband should presume to think

that any spiritual good will be accomplished by his life without an effective ministry of prayer. And no husband may expect an effective prayer life unless he lives with his wife "in an understanding way, bestowing honor" on her. To take the time to maintain a good marriage is God's will; it is serving God; it is a spiritual activity pleasing in His sight.[4]

When a Christian husband hears the phrase "spiritual activity," of what does he immediately think? Prayer? Bible reading? Witnessing? Memorizing Scripture? But does he think of the treatment of his wife as a spiritual activity? In God's eyes, the previously mentioned activities are unproductive if a husband is not growing in knowledge, understanding, and honor toward his wife. By neglecting the commands concerning his role as a husband he cuts off his direct link to the throne of God, interrupting God's response to his prayers.

In contrast, by obeying these commands, husbands ensure for themselves a certain degree of effectiveness in prayer. "For the eyes of the Lord are toward the righteous, and his ears attend to their prayer" (1 Peter 3:12). James 5:16 also instills hope: "The effective prayer of a righteous man can accomplish much." In Peter's mind, a righteous man is a man whose walk of faith is characterized by obedience to God's command to love, honor, and cherish his wife. This is the kind of husband who will see his prayers answered.

When the Holy Spirit prays (Rom. 8:26–27)

We are like foolish children, that are ready to cry for fruit before it is ripe and fit for them.

–Matthew Henry

How do you pray when you don't know what to say? How do you pray when you have lost your Godward perspective, when your hope has been stolen, when you have no joy? How do you pray when you are utterly confused as to what God is doing in and behind your circumstances? When you honestly don't understand what the will of God is? When you are struggling to surrender your own will to God's will? When you have committed the same sin, for the 10,000th time? How do you pray when you don't know what to say?

Questions like these expose the reality that prayer is not easy—it is a struggle. The discipline of prayer is a battle. However, as believers in Jesus Christ we have an all-powerful resource—the Holy Spirit, who prays for us. Romans 8:26–27 explains,

> In the same way the Spirit also helps our weakness; for we do not know how to pray as we should, but the Spirit Himself intercedes for us with groanings too deep for words; and He who searches the hearts knows what the mind of the Spirit is, because He intercedes for the saints according to the will of God.

Here we find massive encouragement to keep praying even when we may not fully understand what exactly we are praying for. Verse 26 begins, "In the same way," which signals that what Paul is about to say connects very closely with the previous context.

Chapter 8 is the completion of a three-chapter section on sanctification, how we grow in Christ. Romans 1–3 exposes our utter depravity and lack of righteousness. Chapters 4–5 explain the gift of God's righteousness, which is ours by repentant faith in Jesus Christ, the second Adam, who came to undo on the cross what the first Adam had done in the garden. Romans 6 describes the right way to win the battle against sin (by recognizing who we are in Christ and daily applying that truth to our heart). Chapter 7 corrects the wrong way to win the battle against sin (by keeping the Law). This is not because the Law is bad; no, the Law is good. The problem is not the Law—it is much deeper.

The problem is the principle of sin reigning in the flesh. This is a deep problem that requires a deeper solution—redemption in Jesus Christ; a redemption that delivers us not only from the eternal penalty of sin, but also from its power in our daily lives. Chapter 8 teaches us how we live out that powerful redemption—by walking according to the Holy Spirit, which is the same as walking according to the Word of God—the book the Spirit wrote.

This battle—the daily fight against the flesh—will continue until the day we see Jesus face to face. Because of this reality, true believers long for the day when they will be fully delivered, fully redeemed. We sing, "Redeemed, how I love to proclaim it …"[1]—we *are already* redeemed.

But we also sing, "When I stand in glory, I will see his face. And there I'll serve my King forever, in that holy place."[2] We *will be* fully redeemed, delivered from the very presence of sin, when we see Christ. Until then, we groan—we ache for the day when our salvation will be complete in our experience.

According to Romans 8:18–22, creation is groaning. All creation feels the effects of the curse and aches for the fullness of redemption. Believers in Christ groan for the redemption of their bodies because the Spirit resides there (v. 23). Then come verses 26–27: "In the same way." Just as creation groans, waiting for the fullness of redemption, and as a believer groans, waiting for redemption from his or her earthly body, so the Holy Spirit groans in prayer: "He who searches the hearts knows what the mind of the Spirit is, because He intercedes for the saints according to the will of God."

In these two verses, we uncover three truths concerning the Holy Spirit's ministry of prayer for us, a ministry which occurs while we continue to war against sin, striving to live out the redemption that is already ours in Christ.

The Holy Spirit prays for us because we are weak (v. 26a)

The Spirit who resides within us "helps" us, that is, He comes to our aid, rescues us, and helps to carry a heavy burden. The same Greek word is used only one other time, in Luke 10:40, when Martha ordered Jesus to tell her sister to help her serve in the kitchen.

Here it speaks of the ongoing ministry of the Spirit of God as he helps us in our "weaknesses," our human frailty, diseases, and infirmities. This includes physical, emotional, and spiritual weakness, which reveal human frailty but do not necessarily result from sin. The word "weakness" is used in other places. Consider two examples:

> And He said to me, "My grace is sufficient for you, for power is perfected in weakness." Most gladly, therefore, I will rather boast about my weaknesses, so that the power of Christ may dwell in me.
>
> 2 Cor. 12:9

> Therefore, since we have a great high priest who has passed through the heavens, Jesus the Son of God, let us hold fast our confession. For we do not have a high priest who cannot sympathize with our weaknesses, but One who has been tempted in all things as we are, yet without sin.
>
> Heb. 4:14–15

Like the hymn writer, we testify, "Jesus knows our every

weakness; take it to the Lord in prayer."³ The Holy Spirit knows our weaknesses too. William R. Newell writes, "The Spirit, who knows the vast abysmal need of every one of us, knows that need to the least possible particular."⁴ This same omniscient Spirit enables us to pray to our Heavenly Father (see Rom. 8:15–17).

The Holy Spirit prays for us because we are ignorant (v. 26b)

We must agree with Paul's testimony, "we do not know how to pray as we should." *Sometimes we are aware of our ignorance.* The disciples said to Jesus, "Lord, teach us to pray" (Luke 11:1). *Sometimes we are blind to our ignorance.* For example, when the sons of Zebedee came to Jesus with their mother to demand that He put them into a position of leadership, Jesus said, "You do not know what you are asking. Are you able to drink the cup that I am about to drink?" (Matt. 20:22). Or, as Paul writes in 2 Corinthians 12:8–9, "Concerning this I implored the Lord three times that it might leave me …" (Paul thought he knew God's plan for his suffering, but he did not). God answered, "My grace is sufficient for you, for power is perfected in weakness."

We need God's grace in our times of weakness. But we also need the Spirit to pray for us because our knowledge is not complete—we are ignorant of some things. Matthew Henry writes, "We are not competent judges of our own condition … We are short-sighted, and very much biased in favour of the flesh, and apt to separate the end from the way … We are like foolish children, that are ready to cry for fruit before it is ripe and fit for them."⁵ One of my young daughters loves to eat pears, but she does not know how to tell when they are ripe. As a result, she will often grab a hard, green pear off the kitchen counter, take one bite, and leave the rest behind, claiming "it is too hard." We often do the same. We want the "fruit" that God is preparing for our future (we may even know what it is), but we want it *now*, before it is ripe and before we are ready. We are ignorant of what is best for us because we are not fully aware of our weakness, and may not be aware of the maturing process God is performing within us. We don't know how to pray as we should. But the Spirit is not ignorant—and He prays for us according to perfect knowledge.

He prays with "groanings too deep for words." A better way to translate this is "wordlessly." The Spirit pleads on our behalf in longings that are inexpressible in words. This is non-verbal prayer. The prayer ministry of the Holy Spirit—His groaning for us—is silent.

The Holy Spirit prays for us because God's knowledge is perfect (v. 27)

The passage continues, "He who searches the hearts knows what the mind of the Spirit is." This speaks of the omniscience of God. When David charged his son Solomon to serve God he reminded him, "the Lord searches all hearts, and understands every intent of the thoughts" (1 Chr. 28:9). To the church at Thyatira, Jesus described Himself as "He who searches the minds and hearts" (Rev. 2:23).

God the Father already knows what the Spirit is thinking. That's why there is no need for the Spirit's groaning to be verbalized. He prays for us "according to the will of God." What great confidence this brings! The Spirit of God knows the thoughts of God (1 Cor. 2:11), and the Father knows the thoughts of the Spirit. This means the two are always in full agreement. Since the thoughts of God are revealed by the Spirit in words (1 Cor. 2:13), His prayers never contradict God's written Word, the Bible. This is crucial for us to understand since we can be guilty of fleshly prayer that is not always in sync with the will of God. R. C. Sproul writes,

> Professing Christians often ask God to bless or sanction their sin. They are even capable of telling their friends they have prayed about a certain matter and God has

given them peace despite what they prayed for was contrary to His will. Such prayers are thinly veiled acts of blasphemy, and we add insult to God when we dare to announce that His Spirit has sanctioned our sin by giving us peace in our souls. Such a peace is a carnal peace and has nothing to do with the peace that passes understanding, the peace that the Spirit is pleased to grant to those who love God and love His law.[6]

Here is where the Spirit helps us immensely. In our ignorance, or even in our fleshly determination to see our own will be done, we often fail to pray according to God's perfect will. We may pray with our mouths, "*Thy* will be done," but mean in our hearts, "*My* will be done." The Holy Spirit does not possess that same inconsistency. He *always* intercedes according to the will of God!

This intercession of the Spirit is only true for believers since the prayer ministry of the Holy Spirit flows out of the ministry of Christ as our Mediator. Several verses later in Romans 8 we read, "Who will bring a charge against God's elect? God is the one who justifies; who is the one who condemns? Christ Jesus is He who died, yes, rather who was raised, who is at the right hand of God, who also intercedes for us" (Rom. 8:33–34). Hebrews 7:25 affirms, "Therefore He is able also to save forever those who draw near to God through Him, since He always lives to make intercession for them."

All three members of the Trinity are actively involved in answering our prayers. The Father turns His ear toward us and listens because He cares for His children. The Son intercedes as our High Priest because He gave His lifeblood to redeem us. The Spirit helps carry our burdens to God. When we do not know how to pray, the Holy Spirit pleads with the Father for us according to His good and perfect will.

This is great incentive to be men and women of prayer. When we are weak and feel we can't go on, the Spirit prays for us. When the battle against indwelling sin has left us completely discouraged, the Spirit intercedes for us. When we are ignorant and we do not even know how to pray, the Spirit silently takes our need to the throne of grace. When our limited understanding wrestles with the will of God, the Spirit prays for us. And He never prays outside the will of God.

What greater assurance of the success of prayer do we need?

Appendixes: Practical helps for cultivating God-dependency

The old saying "More is caught than is taught" is certainly true when it comes to teaching believers how to pray. For this reason, pastors and elders need to model God-dependency in their own lives in order for their sheep to follow their godly example. However, it also means that churches need to continue to find creative ways to go beyond talking about praying to actually praying together—to cultivate the habit of prayer. This section contains a variety of examples of prayer initiatives, prayer-meeting ideas, and other resources that will hopefully spark your own imagination to create fresh ideas.

Appendix 1 is an explanation of an annual prayer event that has proved to be a great blessing to my church family. The "9 Days of Prayer" scheme is a creative way to begin a new year with a concentrated time of prayer.

Appendix 2 contains numerous examples of prayer-service formats. Seasons of prayer are vital in providing spiritual refreshment for the heart of a congregation. Each season lasts approximately one hour.

Appendix 3 is a simple call to keep prayer and evangelism together through cultivating the habit of having a monthly prayer focus on missionary outreach.

Appendix 4 contains an example of how to teach your congregation to pray through passages of Scripture. It is simply one example. I would encourage you to come up with many more that can be directed toward specific needs within your own church family.

Appendix 5 consists of two expository sermon outlines of prayer passages that may easily be developed into short sermons for prayer-meeting instruction, or longer sermons to be preached as part of a regular worship service. God's people never tire of hearing sermons on prayer-related themes.

Appendix 6 contains a Bible study on the topic of God as our heavenly Father who listens to our prayers. I would encourage you to photocopy the study, whether for personal use, or for your small groups or home Bible studies.

Appendix 7 is a call to the pastor to include adequate time for substantial pastoral prayer as part of his church's corporate worship services.

APPENDIX 1. "9 DAYS OF PRAYER"

The desire to cultivate God-dependency in my local church has led to the creation of an annual prayer event. For the past six years, Immanuel Bible Church has conducted what we call "9 Days of Prayer," which begins on the first Saturday in January. Using nine days allows the men to kick off the prayer initiative with a Saturday prayer breakfast, followed later in the day by a ladies' prayer luncheon. This number of days also provides me with two Sundays to preach four different sermons on prayer (morning and evening).

About one month prior to this event all church members and regular attendees receive a form requesting the following information.

- praises from the current year
- prayer requests for the following subjects: areas of life in which spiritual growth is needed, family needs, relationship challenges, and ongoing physical needs
- at least one specific way they would like to see the Lord work in their lives/families during the coming year.

This information is used to design daily prayer sheets which are e-mailed to each family in the congregation. Since new praises and requests are phoned or e-mailed to the church during the nine days, we wait until the event is over before compiling an annual prayer booklet which contains all the praises and requests that have been submitted. This booklet then becomes our congregation's prayer guide for their fellow believers throughout the year. A family's requests may appear in the booklet as something like this (not real names):

JONES, Jim & Mary (Caleb, Joanna, Benjamin, Sue) Praises

- George (Jim's father)—successful cancer surgery; continue to pray for his spiritual needs

- safe delivery of a new baby girl
- salvation of Mary's sister.

Requests

- Sally Smith (Mary's mother)—ongoing battle with cancer, regular chemotherapy
- that we would grow in being bolder witnesses to our unsaved friends and family
- homeschooling challenges
- growth in our family devotion times
- spiritual needs of our children
- faithfulness as parents to raise our children in the nurture and admonition of the Lord
- Jim—growth in spiritual leadership of the home.

In addition to the needs of church families, the prayer booklet contains a section for government leaders, soldiers, the church leadership, current and future ministries of the church, and our missionaries. We also include suggestions of ways to use the booklet throughout the year:

- Page-a-day: pray through the booklet one page per day and then start over again.
- Family of the week: pray for the family of the week as noted on each month's church calendar and in the weekly bulletin.
- Variety: pray for several requests under each category each day.
- Weekly: choose a time to pray over some requests one day per week until you get through the booklet and then start over.
- Small groups: pray through the requests in your Bible study and/or accountability group.
- Be creative: come up with your own practical uses for the booklet.

APPENDIX 2. SEASONS OF PRAYER

Sample 1 (for congregational or small-group use)

Season 1: Admiration

- Scripture readings: 1 Chronicles 29:10–12; Psalm 100:1–5; 34:1–3
- Musical praise: appropriate songs and hymns that exalt God and His attributes
- Sacrifice of praise: prepared or spontaneous testimonies from congregation.

Season 2: Admission

- Scripture readings: Psalm 130:5–6; 19:13–14; 1 John 1:7–9
- Musical plea: a song or hymn that is a prayer of confession and/or plea for cleansing
- Personal confession time: participants bow their heads for silent prayer.

Season 3: Appeal

- Scripture readings: Matthew 7:7; Philippians 4:6–7; James 5:13–16
- Musical prayer: songs and hymns that are written in the form of prayers
- Small-group prayer time.

Season 4: Appreciation

- Scripture readings: Psalm 107:22; Ephesians 3:20–21
- Musical thanksgiving: songs and hymns of praise and thanksgiving
- Closing prayer (by a pastor or elder).

Sample 2 (for congregational or small-group use)

SEASON 1: PROMISE

A season for listening to God's promises, rejoicing, and thanking Him for His faithfulness.

- Scriptures: Psalm 23; Isaiah 30:23; Psalm 81:16; 91:15–16; Proverbs 3:5–6; Lamentations 3:22–23
- Hymns of praise: "How Firm a Foundation";[1] "Speak, O Lord"[2]
- Corporate prayer time; individuals leading as directed by pastor/group leader.

SEASON 2: PENITENCE

A season for soul-searching and confessing sin.

- Scriptures: Nehemiah 1:4–6; Psalm 51:1–5; 66:18; Isaiah 6:5
- Musical plea: "Search Me, O God"[3]
- Personal prayer time for the purpose of confession.

SEASON 3: PETITION

A season for personal requests as well as intercession on behalf of others and the church.

- Scriptures: Matthew 6:25–34; 7:7; 8:26–27; Philippians 4:6–7
- Hymns of petition: "I Need Thee Every Hour";[4] "What a Friend We Have in Jesus"[5]
- Prayer time in groups of two or three.

SEASON 4: PRAISE

A season for expressing gratitude to God for His bountiful blessings and answers to prayer.

- Scriptures: 1 Chronicles 16:7–36; Psalm 107:22; 1 Corinthians 15:57; 1 Thessalonians 5:18
- Songs and hymns of praise: "O God, Our Help in Ages Past";[6] "Great God of Wonders!"[7]
- Corporate praise time, individuals leading in brief sentence prayers of praise.

Sample 3 (for small-group use, without music)

SEASON 1: ADORATION
- Read Psalm 100.
- Spend time praising God for His attributes.

SEASON 2: CONFESSION
- Read Psalm 51. Discuss the words David used that express genuine repentance.
- Spend time in private and/or public confession.

SEASON 3: THANKSGIVING
- Read Psalm 105:1–5.
- Spend time thanking God for specific works He has accomplished.

SEASON 4: SUPPLICATION
- Read Philippians 4:6–8.
- Share prayer needs with one another.
- Spend time praying over the needs expressed by those in the group.

APPENDIX 3. MONTHLY MISSIONARY PRAYER NIGHTS

Prayer is the fuel of missions. This was certainly evident in the early church, as the gospel spread like wildfire and the first missionaries were filled with power and boldness. As missionary evangelists and church planters, the apostles and their co-workers were dependent upon the prayer support of their fellow believers and their supporting churches. As D. A. Carson reminds us, "While William Carey is often referred to as 'the father of modern missions,' it was his sister, bedridden for years, who spent hours each day interceding for the ministry of her brother and for others who were beginning to follow the trail he blazed."[1] Any missionary serving on the frontline of the spiritual war between the true gospel and theological deception knows that his or her ministry will be ineffective without the support of an untold number of "invisible" and unrecognized prayer partners.

For this reason, my church has dedicated one Wednesday evening prayer meeting per month to pray specifically for the work of worldwide missions. In addition to the needs of our "Missionary of the Month," who is prayed for each week, praises and special requests are submitted by all of our missionaries via e-mail. These are then compiled into a prayer list for use on that night. Sometimes a brief ten-to-fifteen-minute Bible lesson on the topic of prayer precedes the time spent in small-group intercession. Other times, our time in prayer is preceded only by congregational singing and Scripture readings. Sometimes our sanctuary is divided into different "continents" representing the locations where our missionaries serve.

The bookmark opposite serves as a handy reminder to people concerning six biblical principles that should influence the way we pray for gospel outreach. A helpful article to distribute among your church family is *Seven Ways to Pray for Your Missionary*, available from OMF International.[2]

HOW TO PRAY FOR GOSPEL OUTREACH

ℰℭ

1. Pray for the Lord to open the hearts of the hearers, just as He did for Lydia (Acts 16:14)

2. Pray for the Lord's victory over Satan's opposition (1 Thes. 2:18; Eph. 6:18)

3. Pray for the witness (Eph. 6:19):
   - to have boldness
   - to be guided in his choice of words

4. Pray for the Holy Spirit's work of conviction and illumination (John 16:8–11; 1 Cor. 2:14)

5. Pray for the power of the gospel to be unleashed (Rom. 1:16; 2 Thes. 3:1)

6. Pray for the drawing power of the Father (John 6:44)

APPENDIX 4. PRAYING SCRIPTURE THROUGH TRIALS

The following suggested prayer is not intended for repetitious use, but is an example of how we may teach fellow believers to pray *through* Scripture. Since the Word of God is the mind of God in written form (1 Cor. 2:10–16), and since the words of our mouths are acceptable to God to the degree that they agree with His Word (Ps. 19:14), then to pray in accordance with Scripture is to pray in the will of God as best we know. It is therefore advantageous to learn to pray God's revealed will back to Him in worship and petition.

The following passage in James is fitting to be prayed back to God in times of trial, thus training believers to anchor their faith to the Word of God and preparing them to respond in worship during their times of trial.

> James, a bond-servant of God and of the Lord Jesus Christ, to the twelve tribes who are dispersed abroad: Greetings. Consider it all joy, my brethren, when you encounter various trials, knowing that the testing of your faith produces endurance. And let endurance have its perfect result, so that you may be perfect and complete, lacking in nothing. But if any of you lacks wisdom, let him ask of God, who gives to all generously and without reproach, and it will be given to him. But he must ask in faith without any doubting, for the one who doubts is like the surf of the sea, driven and tossed by the wind. For that man ought not to expect that he will receive anything from the Lord, being a double-minded man, unstable in all his ways.
>
> James 1:1–8

Here is how a believer may pray this passage of Scripture in worship and supplication.

Praying for yourself when in trial

Father, I know that through faith in Jesus Christ, I am your bond-servant. Therefore, I am not ultimately in charge of my life—You are.

That means You have absolute authority to bring trials into my life in order to test my faith and to help me grow in character, particularly in the quality of endurance.

Therefore, I consciously consider my present trial of _____ as joy, not because the trial itself makes me happy, but because of the confidence I have in Your purpose and wisdom in exalting Christlikeness as a greater treasure than my own personal comfort.

I choose right now to repent of all complaining and ungratefulness of heart.

I confess that sometimes suffering is brought on by my own pride and foolish choices. Help me, therefore, to repent of my errant ways and make whatever changes of heart and habit are needed in my life by the power of the Spirit.

Please use this time of difficulty to produce in me an enduring will, and let that stamina bring me closer to becoming mature in Christ, lacking nothing that I essentially need in order to live for the glory of your redeeming grace.

I confess that I lack wisdom to make the right decisions in this time of testing. Instead, I find myself being rash and impulsive, motivated more by worry, for the sake of temporary relief. So I am claiming Your promise to give wisdom not sparingly but in truckloads, so that I may please You and not myself.

I confess that, though I know I should have strong faith, I am often like the father who came to Jesus on behalf of his mute son, saying, "I do believe; help my unbelief" [Mark 9:24].

I know my faith should be strong, but sometimes I am so weak. Help me trust You completely and not go back and forth from belief to doubt, from doubt to belief, like the moving waters of the ocean upon the sandy beach. For I know you cannot reward unbelief, since it is impossible to please You without faith [Heb. 11:6].

Help me to be solid and stable in my faith so that I may not rightly be called "double-minded."

Above all, help me to submit to this present trial so that I may become like Jesus Christ [Rom. 8:29], my Lord and Savior, and that by watching my response to suffering, others may see Him in me … all for the glory of His name. Amen.

Praying for others who are experiencing trials

Father, I know that through faith in Jesus Christ, _____ is your bond-servant. Therefore, help _____ to remember that he/she is not ultimately in charge of his/her life—You are.

That means You have absolute authority to bring trials into _____'s life in order to test his/her faith and help him/her grow in the character quality of endurance.

Therefore, help _____ to consciously consider his/her present trial as joy, not because the trial itself makes him/her happy, but because of the confidence that I have in Your purpose and wisdom in exalting Christlikeness as a greater treasure than our own personal comfort.

Help _____ to choose right now to repent of all complaining and ungratefulness of heart.

I confess that I do not know if _____'s present trial is the natural consequence of any pride or foolish choices he/she has made. But if that is the case, help him/her to repent of those sins and make whatever changes of heart and habit are needed in his/her life by the power of the Spirit.

Please use this time of difficulty to produce in _____ an enduring will, and let that endurance bring him/her closer to becoming mature in Christ, lacking nothing that he/she essentially needs in order to live for Your glory.

I confess that I often lack wisdom to make the right decisions in times of testing. Instead, I can be rash and impulsive, motivated more by worry, for the sake of temporary relief. So I am claiming Your promise to give wisdom to _____ not sparingly but in truckloads, so that he/she may please You and not himself/herself.

I confess that, though we know we should have strong faith, we are often like the father who came to Jesus on behalf of his mute son, saying, "I do believe; help my unbelief" [Mark 9:24].

I know our faith should always be strong, but sometimes we are so weak. Help_____ to trust You completely and not go back and forth from belief to doubt, from doubt to belief, like the moving waters of the ocean upon the sandy beach. Help _____ to remember that You cannot reward unbelief, since it is impossible to please You without faith [Heb. 11:6].

Help _____ to be solid and stable in his/her faith so that he/she may not rightly be called "double-minded."

Above all, help _____ to learn to submit to this present trial so that he/she may become like Jesus Christ, the Lord and Savior [Rom. 8:29], and that by watching his/her response to suffering, others may see Him … all for the glory of His name. Amen.

APPENDIX 5. TWO PRAYER-SERMON OUTLINES

An Old Testament outline

Title: Six Elements of Compelling Prayer
Text: Nehemiah 1:4–11

- Compassion for those in need (v. 4)
- Confidence in God's character (v. 5)
- Contriteness of spirit (v. 6a)
- Confession of known sin (vv. 6b–7)
- Commitment to God's Word (vv. 8–10)
- Call for specific intercession (v. 11)

A New Testament outline

Title: God uses thankful prayer to accomplish His work
Text: Philippians 1:3–11

- Thankful prayer stems from confident assurance (vv. 3–6)
- Thankful prayer stirs up godly affections (vv. 7–8)
- Thankful prayer strives for fruitful affluence (vv. 9–11)

APPENDIX 6. SMALL-GROUP BIBLE STUDY ON PRAYER

You are encouraged to photocopy this Bible study for small-group use.

Praying to the Father who listens

Complete the following Bible study in a small-group discussion. Then spend time in prayer together.

1. How is God described in the following verses: Psalm 91:15; Matthew 6:6; James 1:17?

2. How did Jesus instruct us to address God? Why is this privilege for believers only? See Matthew 6:9; Matthew 18:19; 1 John.

3. What are some of the conditions for effective prayer? Look at 2 Chronicles 7:14; Jeremiah 29:13; Mark 11:24; John 15:7; 1 Thessalonians 5:17; James 5:16; 1 John 3:22.

4. Read 2 Corinthians 12:8–9. What is one reason why God does not answer our prayers as we desire?

5. What causes God to turn a deaf ear to our prayers? Study Psalm 66:18; Isaiah 59:1–2; Proverbs 1:28–30; 1 Peter 3:7; James 4:3; James 1:6–8.

6. Read Matthew 6:5–15. What are the essential elements in a biblical pattern of prayer?

APPENDIX 7. PASTORAL PRAYER AS PART OF CORPORATE WORSHIP

As evangelical churches become increasingly user-friendly in an attempt to reach their world for Christ, one of the aspects of corporate worship that has fallen on hard times is what is customarily known as the *pastoral prayer*. This longer time of prayer (about five minutes in my church) is a very important part of my local church's worship, a time during which I lead my flock to God's throne of grace (Heb. 4:14–16). For the believers, it has become a singular time of communion with God as they affirm in their hearts, and perhaps discreetly with their voices, the praise, thanksgiving, and supplications that are brought to God's ears. For the unbelievers, this longer time of prayer may make them feel uncomfortable (visitors have commented as much), but there is no reason to apologize for that. Church is for the church—if we understand the Bible correctly. This does not mean we go out of our way to offend unbelievers, since we ought always to show them the gracious love of Christ. But we certainly must not "design" our worship services with unregenerate desires in mind. To do so is to abandon a biblical ecclesiology.

The ministry of James Montgomery Boice, the late pastor of Tenth Presbyterian Church in Philadelphia, was characterized by an intense love for the corporate worship of the church. *Give Praise to God: A Vision for Reforming Worship* is a book written by a number of his friends and ministry peers. In a chapter entitled "Does God Care How We Worship?" Ligon Duncan cites Boice's concern for the growing absence of substantial prayer in church worship services, particularly the passing away of the "pastoral prayer":

> It is almost inconceivable to me that something called worship can be held without any significant prayer, but

that is precisely what is happening. There is usually a short prayer at the beginning of the service, though even that is fading away. It is being replaced with a chummy greeting to make people feel welcome and at ease. Sometimes people are encouraged to turn around and shake hands with those who are next to them in the pews. Another prayer that is generally retained is the prayer for the offering. We can understand that, since we know that it takes the intervention of Almighty God to get self-centered people to give enough money to keep the church running. But longer prayers—pastoral prayers—are vanishing. Whatever happened to the acts acrostic in which *a* stands for adoration, *c* for confession of sin, *t* for thanksgiving, and *s* for supplication? There is no rehearsal of God's attributes or confession of sin against the shining, glorious background of God's holiness.

And what happens when Mary Jones is going to have an operation and the people know it and think she should be prayed for? Quite often prayers for people like that are tacked onto the offering prayer, because there is no other spot for them in the service. How can we say we are worshiping when we do not even pray?[1]

In response to this question, every serious pastor needs to take time to study and to meditate on the Apostle Paul's pastoral prayers, such as Colossians 1:9–14; Philippians 1:9–11; or Ephesians 3:14–21. From this study, we quickly conclude that Paul's shepherding heart moved him to intercede regularly for the needs of his people. A helpful aid in this study is D. A. Carson's book *A Call to Spiritual Reformation*.[2]

My fellow ministers, if you already faithfully bring your sheep to the Lord in the name of Jesus, the Good Shepherd, remain steadfast in what is a biblically warranted aspect of public worship. God's people will learn to pray, at least partially, by listening to you pray for them. If you have not practiced this discipline, please begin this coming Sunday. You, and your people, will be so glad you did.

ENDNOTES

Introduction

1 R. L. Dabney, *Lectures in Systematic Theology* (Grand Rapids, MI: Baker, 1985), p. 713.

2 Ibid., p. 720.

Chapter 1

1 Robert Duncan Culver, *Systematic Theology* (Fearn: Mentor/Christian Focus, 2005), p. 731.

2 See Homer A. Kent, Jr., *Jerusalem to Rome* (Winona Lake, IN: BMH Books, 1972), p. 25.

3 Kenneth O. Gangel, and Max Anders, (ed.), *Acts: Holman New Testament Commentary* (Nashville: Holman Reference, 1998), p. 12.

4 J. C. Ryle, *A Call to Prayer* (Edinburgh: Banner of Truth, 2002), p. 7.

Chapter 2

1 Martin Luther, cited at: quotationsbook.com.

2 Fritz Rienecker and Cleon Rogers, *Linguistic Key to the Greek New Testament* (Grand Rapids, MI: Zondervan, 1976), p. 603.

3 A. W. Pink, *The Sovereignty of God* (1930; 1995, Grand Rapids, MI: Baker), p. 176.

4 Lehman Straus, *Sense and Nonsense about Prayer* (Chicago: Moody Press, 1974), p. 24.

5 John Piper, *The Pleasures of God* (Sisters, OR: Multnomah, 2000), pp. 225–227.

6 Jerry Bridges, *The Practice of Godliness* (Colorado Springs: NavPress, 1983), pp. 124–125.

Part 2

1 Henry C. Thiessen, *Lectures in Systematic Theology* (Grand Rapids, MI: Eerdmans, 1949), p. 302.

Chapter 3

1 Ryle, *A Call to Prayer*, p. 11.

2 William MacDonald, *Believer's Bible Commentary* (Nashville: Thomas Nelson, 1995), p. 1731.

3 Dabney, *Lectures in Systematic Theology*, p. 716.

Chapter 5

1 Alex Montoya, "Approaching Pastoral Ministry Scripturally," in John MacArthur, (ed.), *Rediscovering Pastoral Ministry* (Dallas: Word, 1995), p. 81.

Chapter 6

1 Straus, *Sense and Nonsense about Prayer*, p. 101.

Chapter 7

1 J. Oswald Sanders, *Spiritual Leadership* (Chicago: Moody Press, 1967), p. 121.

2 Ryle, *A Call to Prayer*, p. 4.

3 The Bible recognizes the place of true medicine in our lives: Jesus treated the presence of medical doctors as one of the realities of our living in sin-cursed bodies (Matt. 9:12), and the Apostle Paul had a medical doctor, Luke, as his traveling companion and personal attendant (Col. 4:14; 2 Tim. 4:11). However, some illnesses should also induce believers to call their pastor-elders for anointing and prayer, according to the instruction of James 5:13–16, so that the possibility of the presence of a sin-cause can be gently confronted, resulting in biblical confession. The Scriptures warn us not to seek the help of physicians in place of seeking help from the Lord (2 Chr. 16:12).

4 B. B. Warfield, *Counterfeit Miracles* (1918; 1995, Edinburgh: Banner of Truth), pp. 171–172, 199.

5 Ryle, *A Call to Prayer*, p. 28.

6 Iain Murray, *Pentecost—Today?* (Edinburgh: Banner of Truth, 1998), p. 69.

7 D. Edmond Hiebert, *James* (Chicago: Moody Press, 1979), p. 299.

8 Christopher W. Morgan and B. Dale Ellenburg, *James: Wisdom for the Community* (Focus on the Bible; Fearn: Christian Focus, 2008), p. 203.

9 C. H. Spurgeon, "Extraordinary Thought-Reading," *Sword & Trowel*, 3 (2003), p. 16.

Chapter 8

1 J. N. D. Kelly, *The Epistles of Peter and of Jude* (Peabody, MA: Hendrickson, 1969), p. 133.

2 Kenneth S. Wuest, *Wuest's Word Studies: First Peter* (Grand Rapids, MI: Eerdmans, 1942), p. 83.

3 Ibid., p. 83.

4 John Piper and Wayne Grudem, (eds.), *Recovering Biblical Manhood and Womanhood* (Wheaton, IL: Crossway, 1991), p. 208.

Chapter 9

1 Fanny J. Crosby, "Redeemed" (1882).

2 Melody Green, "There Is a Redeemer" (1982).

3 Joseph Scriven, "What a Friend We Have in Jesus" (1855).

4 William R. Newell, *Romans* (Chicago: Moody Press, 1938), p. 326.

5 Matthew Henry, *Matthew Henry's Commentary on the Whole Bible,* vol. vi (McLean, VA: MacDonald [n.d.]), p. 422.

6 R. C. Sproul, *The Invisible Hand* (Phillipsburg, NJ: P&R, 2003), p. 209.

Appendix 2

1 "K" in John Rippon's Selection of Hymns, "How Firm a Foundation" (1787).

2 Keith Getty and Stuart Townend, "Speak, O Lord," 2005.

3 J. Edwin Orr, "Search Me, O God" (1912–1987).

4 Annie S. Hawks, "I Need Thee Every Hour" (1872).

5 Joseph M. Scriven, "What a Friend We Have in Jesus" (1855).

6 Isaac Watts, "O God, Our Help in Ages Past" (1719).

7 Samuel Davies, "Great God of Wonders!" (published posthumously, 1769).

Appendix 3

1 D. A. Carson, *A Call to Spiritual Reformation: Priorities from Paul and his Prayers* (Grand Rapids, MI: Baker, 1992), p. 123.

2 "Seven Ways to Pray for Your Missionary," available at: omf.org/omf/us/resources__1/prayer_resources.

Appendix 7

1 James Montgomery Boice, cited by J. Ligon Duncan III, "Does God Care How We Worship?" in Philip Graham Ryken, Derek W. H. Thomas, and J. Ligon Duncan III, (eds.), *Give Praise to God: A Vision for Reforming Worship* (Phillipsburg, NJ: P&R, 2003), pp. 18–19.

2 D. A. Carson, *A Call to Spiritual Reformation: Priorities from Paul and his Prayers* (Grand Rapids, MI: Baker, 1992).

FOR FURTHER HELP AND INFORMATION

Books to strengthen prayer ministry

Bennett, Arthur, (ed.), *The Valley of Vision* (Edinburgh: Banner of Truth, 1975).

Bounds, E. M., *The Complete Works of E. M. Bounds on Prayer* (Grand Rapids, MI: Baker, 1999).

Bunyan, John, *Prayer* (Puritan Paperback; Edinburgh: Banner of Truth, 1965).

Carson, D. A., *A Call to Spiritual Reformation: Priorities from Paul and His Prayers* (Grand Rapids, MI: Baker, 1992).

Deyneka, Peter, *Much Prayer—Much Power* (Grand Rapids, MI: Zondervan, 1958).

Eastman, Dick, *The Hour that Changes the World* (Grand Rapids, MI: Baker, 1978).

Elliff, Tom, *A Passion for Prayer* (Wheaton, IL: Crossway, 1998).

MacArthur, John, *Alone with God* (Wheaton, IL: Victor, 1995).

Mack, Wayne, *Reaching the Ear of God* (Phillipsburg, NJ: P&R, 2004).

Ryken, Philip Graham, *When You Pray* (Phillipsburg, NJ: P&R, 2006).

Ryle, J. C., *A Call to Prayer* (Edinburgh: Banner of Truth, 2002).

Sproul, R. C., *The Prayer of the Lord* (Orlando, FL: Reformation Trust, 2009).

Straus, Lehman, *Sense and Nonsense about Prayer* (Chicago: Moody, 1981).

Weems, Reggie, *On Wings of Prayer* (Leominster: Day One, 2009)

Books to strengthen pastoral ministry

Adams, Jay E., *A Call to Discernment* (Eugene, OR: Harvest House, 1987).

——*Shepherding God's Flock* (Grand Rapids, MI: Zondervan, 1974).

Baxter, Richard, *The Reformed Pastor* (1656; 1974, Edinburgh: Banner of Truth).

Burroughs, Jeremiah, *Gospel Fear* (1647; 1991, Orlando, FL: Soli Deo Gloria).

Dever, Mark, *Nine Marks of a Healthy Church* (Wheaton, IL: Crossway, 2004).

Duncan, J. Ligon, and Hunt, Susan, *Women's Ministry in the Local Church* (Wheaton, IL: Crossway, 2006).

Elliff, Tom, *A Passion for Prayer* (Wheaton, IL: Crossway, 1998).

Kuiper, R. B., *God-Centred Evangelism* (London: Banner of Truth, 1966).

Lloyd-Jones, D. Martyn, *What Is an Evangelical?* (Edinburgh: Banner of Truth, 1992).

MacArthur, John, *The Master's Plan for the Church* (Chicago: Moody, 1991).

——and the Master's Seminary Faculty, *Rediscovering Pastoral Ministry* (Dallas: Word, 1995).

Murray, Iain, *Evangelicalism Divided* (Edinburgh: Banner of Truth, 2000).

Nettles, Thomas J., *By His Grace and For His Glory* (Lake Charles, LA: Cor Meum Tibi, 2002).

Piper, John, *Brothers, We are Not Professionals* (Nashville: B&H, 2002).

Sanders, J. Oswald, *Spiritual Leadership* (Chicago: Moody, 1967).

Schreiner, Thomas R., *Paul: Apostle of God's Glory in Christ* (Downers Grove, IL: InterVarsity Press, 2001).

Shaw, John, *The Character of a Pastor according to God's Heart* (Ligonier, PA: Soli Deo Gloria, 1992).

Spurgeon, Charles H., *An All-Round Ministry* (Pasadena, TX: Pilgrim, 1983).

Strauch, Alexander, *Biblical Eldership* (Littleton, CO: Lewis & Roth, 1986).

——*The New Testament Deacon* (Littleton, CO: Lewis & Roth, 1992).

Tautges, Paul, *Comfort Those Who Grieve* (Leominster: Day One, 2009).

——*Counsel One Another* (Leominster: Day One, 2009).

——*Counsel Your Flock* (Leominster: Day One, 2009).

Thomas, Curtis C., *Life in the Body of Christ* (Cape Coral, FL: Founders Press, 2006).

Watson, Thomas, *A Body of Divinity* (1692; 1965, London: Banner of Truth).

Webster, Douglas D., *Selling Jesus* (Downers Grove, IL: IVP, 1992).

Wells, David F., *The Courage to Be Protestant* (Grand Rapids, MI: Eerdmans, 2008).

——*God in the Wasteland* (Grand Rapids, MI: Eerdmans, 1994).

——*No Place for Truth* (Grand Rapids, MI: Eerdmans, 1993).

Also available

Counsel one another
A theology of personal discipleship

PAUL TAUTGES

192PP, PAPERBACK

ISBN 978-1-84625-142-9

Today, churches are increasingly placing their confidence in Christian psychology as the answer to their need for the ministry of counseling. But counseling is not primarily the work of the professional: it is a crucial way for believers in Christ to demonstrate biblical love toward one another within a gospel-centered, truth-driven, and grace-dispensing church environment. That is the main point of this book.

Solidly rooted in the belief that the Scriptures are sufficient for every soul-related struggle in life, and totally committed to the truth that the Holy Spirit is competent to accomplish the work of sanctification, this paradigm-shifting book will challenge every believer.

In his companion work, *Counsel Your Flock*, Paul concentrated on the role that teaching shepherds have in leading God's people to spiritual maturity by faithfully equipping them for effective ministry. Here he biblically presents, and thoroughly defends, every believer's responsibility to work toward God's goal to conform us to the image of His Son—a goal that will not be reached apart from a targeted form of discipleship, most often referred to as "counseling."

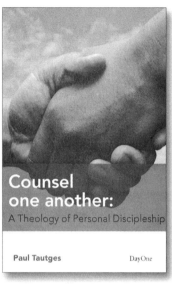

'This book gets it right! Comprehensive and convincing, Counsel One Another shows how true biblical counseling and preaching fit hand-in-glove. Those who preach, teach, or counsel regularly are sure to benefit greatly from this helpful resource.'

JOHN MACARTHUR, PASTOR-TEACHER OF GRACE COMMUNITY CHURCH, SUN VALLEY, CALIFORNIA; AUTHOR; AND BIBLE TEACHER ON THE GRACE TO YOU RADIO PROGRAM

'How refreshing—and rare—to see a book like this that asserts the irresistible power of God's Word to develop true discipleship by the sovereign working of His Spirit. This is not a 'trendy book' like so many, blown about by the prevailing evangelical winds. Rather, here is an anchor for authentic ministry that will stimulate real spiritual growth in God's people. May the Lord set an open door before this book and use it to affect the lives of many.'

DR. STEVEN J. LAWSON, SENIOR PASTOR, CHRIST FELLOWSHIP BAPTIST CHURCH, MOBILE, ALABAMA

Also available

Counsel your flock
Fulfilling your role as a teaching shepherd

PAUL TAUTGES

96PP, PAPERBACK

ISBN 978-1-84625-154-2

The ministry of counseling has for too long been relegated to the professional counselor. Paul Tautges brings the biblical command for discipleship right back to the local church and to all believers. Rather than send people who are struggling spiritually, socially, and emotionally to a limited group of professionals, Tautges makes the case theologically that the responsibility for all church members is to disciple one another and to restore hurting people.

In this companion to his previous book, *Counsel One Another*, he makes it clear that for this one-another ministry to take place it is essential that pastors understand the key role that they play in the discipleship process. Believers need a way to measure their pastor's discipleship philosophy and skills and pastors need a way to teach them to be involved in the counseling, discipleship, restoring-one-another ministry.

'This book gets it right! Comprehensive and convincing, *Counsel Your Flock* shows how true biblical counseling and preaching fit hand-in-glove. Those who preach, teach, or counsel regularly are sure to benefit greatly from this helpful resource.'

DR. JOHN MACARTHUR, PASTOR-TEACHER OF GRACE COMMUNITY CHURCH IN SUN VALLEY, CALIFORNIA

'The ministry of counseling has for too long been relegated to the professional counselor. Paul Tautges brings the biblical command for discipleship right back to the local church and to all believers.

This is a book about local church discipleship, of which leadership is a big part. *Counsel Your Flock* addresses an important need. This is a must read!'

DR. RON ALLCHIN, EXECUTIVE DIRECTOR OF THE BIBLICAL COUNSELING CENTER IN ARLINGTON HEIGHTS, ILLINOIS

Also available

Comfort those who grieve
Ministering God's grace in times of loss

PAUL TAUTGES

144PP, PAPERBACK

ISBN 978-1-84625-155-9

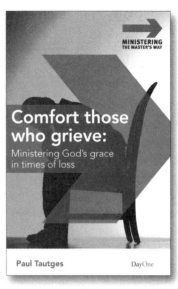

Paul Tautges   DayOne

Until the end of time, when the curse of sin is finally removed, suffering will be a large part of the human experience—and a large part of that suffering will be walking through the painful reality of death. Death is not foreign territory that ministers of grace walk upon. As a result, "Death," writes Paul Tautges, "provides a natural opportunity not only for ministry to others, but also for personal growth in ministers." Therefore, church shepherds must not waste these precious and painful occasions that God provides for the demonstration of mercy and the advantage of the gospel.

This book is a treasure chest of pastoral theology that will equip ministers to reach out to those who grieve with the Christ-centered comfort of God rooted in the gospel. The theological foundation espoused here, as well as the numerous practical helps that are included, will help any servant of the Lord to point the hearts and minds of the bereaved to the "man of sorrows" who is "acquainted with grief" (Isa. 53:3).

'I know of no book like *Comfort Those Who Grieve*. We are given concrete ideas for consoling those who are dying and then on preparing funeral messages which not only comfort the grieving, but also challenge the lost with a clear gospel message. Most "how to" books are shallow and often devoid of deep theological content. This excellent book is an exception.'

CURTIS C. THOMAS, PASTOR FOR OVER FIFTY YEARS, BIBLE TEACHER, AND AUTHOR OF LIFE IN THE BODY

'Few have attempted to offer comfort to those who grieve, and fewer have been as successful ... I commend this wonderful little volume. It is an important tool which should be thoughtfully read if we are to minister wisely and effectively to those in our fellowship who will eventually face such times.'

DR. WALTER C. KAISER, JR., PRESIDENT EMERITUS, GORDON-CONWELL THEOLOGICAL SEMINARY, HAMILTON, MASSACHUSETTS, USA

About Day One:

Day One's threefold commitment:
- To be faithful to the Bible, God's inerrant, infallible Word;
- To be relevant to our modern generation;
- To be excellent in our publication standards.

I continue to be thankful for the publications of Day One. They are biblical; they have sound theology; and they are relevant to the issues at hand. The material is condensed and manageable while, at the same time, being complete—a challenging balance to find. We are happy in our ministry to make use of these excellent publications.

JOHN MACARTHUR, PASTOR-TEACHER, GRACE COMMUNITY CHURCH, CALIFORNIA

It is a great encouragement to see Day One making such excellent progress. Their publications are always biblical, accessible and attractively produced, with no compromise on quality. Long may their progress continue and increase!

JOHN BLANCHARD, AUTHOR, EVANGELIST AND APOLOGIST

Visit our web site for more information and
to request a free catalogue of our books.

www.dayone.co.uk

North American web site—
www.dayonebookstore.com